AZTLAN
THE SOUTHWEST
AND ITS PEOPLES

AZTLAN

THE SOUTHWEST
AND ITS PEOPLES

Luis F. Hernandez

Associate Dean, School of Education
California State University, Northridge

613148

HAYDEN BOOK COMPANY, INC.
Rochelle Park, New Jersey

To
mi corazón, Jeanne
and
the Chicanos of Aztlán

Library of Congress Cataloging in Publication Data

Hernandez, Luis F.
 Aztlán, the Southwest and its peoples.

 Includes index.
  1. Southwest, New—History. 2. Mexican Americans—
Southwest, New—History. I. Title.
F799.H45   917.9′06′6872   74-31039
ISBN 0-8104-5521-8
ISBN 0-8104-5520-X (pbk.)

Printed in the United States of America

1	2	3	4	5	6	7	8	9	PRINTING

75 76 77 78 79 80 81 82   YEAR

Contents

INTRODUCTION
The Beginning 1

CHAPTER 1:   THE SEVEN CITIES OF CIBOLA

Part I—The Dream
Explorers of Aztlán 6
Adventure to Cíbola 11
Part II—The Conquest of Cíbola
Other Expeditions 15

CHAPTER 2:   GOLD AND GOD

Part I—The Continuing Search
Expansion of the Northern Frontier 30
Efforts to Colonize 34
Part II—First Permanent Colony
A Pioneering Colonist 36
Carretas Move Northward 37
The Royal Town of Santa Fe 41
Popé the Pueblo Leader 44
More Indian Confrontation 47

CHAPTER 3:   NORTHWARD MOVEMENT

Part I—Father Eusebio Francisco Kino
Pimería Alta 51
Part II—Alta California
Men of Accomplishment 57
The California Indians 61
Newcomers Settle 62
Part III—Tejas
Slow Progress in Tejas 66
Political Maneuvering 68

CHAPTER 4:   A NEW CULTURE

Arts and Crafts 71
Poetry, Songs and Ballads 73
Cattle Ranching 76
The Vaquero 77

Land Holdings 78
Administrative Bureaucracy 80
Three More Government Agencies 81

CHAPTER 5: STRANGERS FROM THE EAST

Part I—Early Visitors
Growing Territorial Threats 83
Revolutionary Activities 86
Cultural Differences 90

Part II—More Strangers from the East
Trappers and Traders 95
Mounting Pressure for Statehood 98
Other Battles 102

CHAPTER 6: THE SOUTHWEST

Part I—War with the United States
Causes for War 103
Territories Annexed 105
The Californios 112
The Treaty of Guadalupe Hidalgo 115
The Gold Rush 117

Part II—The Conqueror and the Conquered
The Apaches 123
Land Grant Claims 126
The Gringo and the Greaser 129

CHAPTER 7: THE MEXICAN AMERICAN

Part I—To Become a Minority
The Barrio 136
Migrant Labor 140
Jesús Pallares 147
Braceros and Agribusiness 149
A New Self Image 153

Part II—The Mexican American Today—The Chicano Generation
Advocates of La Raza 158
Cesar Chavez and Huelga 162
Community Organizations 168

Suggested Activities 173

Index 177

Introduction

THE BEGINNING

The history of many places has had its beginning in legend. So it is with the Southwest. Many centuries before the white man came to the New World, the people who lived in the Southwest (which was then called Aztlán) were told to travel south. They were told to leave Aztlán and to seek a more friendly and fertile land. These people were the Nahua, forefathers of the Aztecs. Their gods, speaking through their wise men in the Nahuatl language, told them to travel south until they saw an eagle devouring a serpent. This sign would tell them that they had found the place where the land was friendlier and more fertile. The Nahua did as they were told. Where they finally saw the eagle devouring the serpent they built a new city, which they named Tenochtitlán. Tenochtitlán today is known as Mexico City.

The legend says that not all the people of Aztlán went south; many stayed behind. Their lands today are that portion of the United States consisting of California, Arizona, New Mexico, Texas, Nevada, Utah, and parts of Wyoming, Colorado, Kansas, and Oklahoma. The greater portion of this vast area is today's Southwest.

1

The history of the Southwest is not simply the story of what happened to people in a specific geographical area. It is an interpretation of people's actions and reactions to the forces that moved their lives. Nature, of course, has been an important force. Other forces that have caused man to act and react are those that he has created himself. Man has changed the surface of the land in his attempt to hold water for irrigation. He has built roads, cities, harbors, and industrial centers. He has dug deep into the earth for the mineral wealth hidden there; he has used these minerals to build, to create, to change further the surface of the land. The strong have forced their fellow men to take up new forms of worship, new laws and customs, new technology. By so doing man has destroyed cultures that had existed for centuries, turning upside down the lives of their peoples. Often, man has used violence to accomplish what he felt was important; in an attempt to help his own people, he has disregarded the rights and way of life of others.

To interpret the history of the Southwest is to tell the story of the actions and reactions to such forces by five distinctly different groups of people: the Indian, the Spaniard, the Mexican, the Anglo American, and the Mexican American. In closely related ways, each of these groups has played a major part in the development of the Southwest. During a period of about 400 years, the Indians were defenders; the Spaniards were explorers and conquerors; the Mexicans, settlers; the Anglo Americans, second conquerors and settlers; and the Mexican Americans, the builders and blenders. The actions and reactions of one group to another have sometimes been without conflict. Often terrible clashes between them have brought great destruction, terror and death. Yet there has been a constant exchange of ideas among all the people. Some groups have feared that changes would cause them to lose their identity; while absorbing new ideas they have held on strongly to their cultures. They have refused to abandon their ways of life for those of another.

Nevertheless, a new culture developed in the Southwest. The Indian and the Spanish intermingled, creating a people that contrast sharply with those that had existed before—the Mexican. Mexicans are said to be a *mestizo* people. *Mestizo* is the Spanish word for a person who is created from the mixture of two cultures.

For 250 years the Indian, the Spaniard, and the Mexican lived together, each making its special contributions to the development of the Southwest. For example, the Spaniards brought the horse to the Southwest. The horse was the main reason that the Spaniards readily conquered the Indians, for it made the mounted Spanish soldier a stronger and more able fighter. Later, the Indians found that the horse made it possible to hunt the buffalo on the run with a lance rather than with an arrow that had to hit a fatal spot. Still later, the horse helped the Indian to resist better the invading white man. From the Indians the Spaniards learned about irrigation. The Indians also showed the newcomers what plant life they could use to ease their thirst.

As time passed, the *mestizo* culture began to stand out more clearly as the product of two cultures, making a distinct contribution. For example, in a part of culture as simple as food, one can taste the richness of the mixture. Corn formed the base of most Indian food. A typical form of Indian bread made from corn is the *tortilla*. *Tortillas* are often filled with beef (Spanish food), prepared in a chili and tomato sauce (Indian food), and served with *frijoles* (Indian food: beans) and rice (Spanish food) on the side. It would not be difficult to make a long list of such examples.

Not until two and one-half centuries after the establishment of the first colony in New Mexico does the Anglo American appear as a cultural force in the Southwest. (This Spanish colony was founded on August 18, 1598, and was called San Juan Bautista. The founding of San Juan predates that of Jamestown in 1607 by about 10 years, and the landing of the Pilgrims by more than 20 years.) The Anglo Americans who came to the Southwest did not always make themselves part of what they found. Instead, most of them continued the Anglo-American way of life they had brought with them. For example, the houses they built were like those they had left behind in the Northeast, with sharply pitched roofs. In the desert lands, such buildings were out of place and uncomfortable. The Anglo Americans at first made many mistakes. Not understanding the climate, they planted in areas that were washed away by flash floods. Flash floods occur when the rain falls so hard and fast that the earth cannot absorb it. Like a giant wave, the water rushes down river beds and over fields, carrying away everything in its path.

But little by little, the Anglo Americans learned from the cultures they found in the Southwest, adopting what seemed important to them. While they did not unite with the ways of life they found, they did adapt enough so that it became easy to tell a westerner from an easterner.

The Mexican American was different from the other four cultures. In the label that is used to identify him is told the story of his composition. The "Mexican" in Mexican American indicates that he possesses a separate and a mixed Indian and Spanish heritage and culture. The "American" in Mexican American shows that his culture possesses a great deal of what is called "the American way of life." This bringing together of four cultures into one people has made the Mexican American unique.

Today, the Mexican American is aware of his uniqueness and is trying to make other people recognize those characteristics and qualities that make him and his culture different. As has been pointed out, culture is "a way of life" that includes all aspects of daily living as well as the material things, such as tools and artifacts, needed to maintain a mode of living. It also includes language, religion, art; morals—the code of behavior by which people live; values—those aspects of life to which people attach great importance; and traditions—beliefs and practices handed down from generation to generation. People who follow the same way of life, therefore, can be said to have a common culture.

Many people believe that their own culture provides the only true way to live. Yet other cultures offer different points of view, different ways of life, different ways of solving problems, raising children, earning a living, or worshipping God. Cultural conflicts are generally created when one culture refuses to be taken over or changed by another. Europeans came to the New World expecting to find a people equal to themselves. Instead they found cultures that had yet to achieve what the European considered to be the outward signs of a "civilized" people. The Europeans thus looked down on the cultures they found, labeling them "barbarian" or savage.

The Spaniards set out to "civilize" the various Indian cultures. First, Indians were forced into towns. They had to adopt a system of government and a social structure that resembled town life in Spain. Second, they had to dress in the Spanish manner. Men were required to wear trousers and shirts and women to wear skirts and upper garments. Third, the Indian men were forced to practice "monogamy," marriage to one woman, and to celebrate that marriage with formal Christian ceremonies. Finally, Indians were expected to live in stone or adobe houses, to learn the Spanish language, and to abandon many of the customs, traditions, and values of their own cultures. Although the degree to which these standards were enforced varied from place to place, it is generally true that the Spaniards severely disrupted native cultures. It is also generally true that the more powerful culture will see itself as being superior and will force its way of life on weaker people the world over.

Another cause for cultural conflict has been economic expansion —taking over another land and its people either for the labor they can produce or for the yield of their land. Wealth is necessary to a nation's strength. It provides a form of guarantee that an established government or group will continue in control. Expansion also involves securing strategic positions for defense. In other words, a nation needs to build defenses to protect its sources of wealth.

More than any place else in the United States, the Southwest has been a center for cultural "hold-outs." Some cultures have refused to band together and have resisted being absorbed by more powerful forces. Examples of such hold-outs are many, especially among the Indians and the Mexicans, even though all cultural groups in this vast area have freely exchanged and adapted aspects of living over the centuries.

Among the people who figure in the story of the Southwest are some fascinating individuals: the "conquerors," who sought the wealth that might provide them and their rulers with power; the "defenders," who struggled to protect what they considered to be most important, be it their identity or their property; the "builders," who came with invaders and brought with them what they considered to be the best of their particular way of life.

1

The Seven Cities of Cibola

PART I—THE DREAM

Explorers of Aztlán

The first Europeans to see any part of the Southwest were Alonso Alvarez de Piñeda and the crewmen of the four caravels he commanded. The event took place in 1519, 27 years after Columbus' voyage to the New World. Piñeda and his crew had sailed northwest from the island of Jamaica looking for a passageway to the Orient. In his search he located the mouth of the Mississippi River. He and his men also were the first Europeans to see the coast of Texas, although they did not land.

Piñeda was followed by other explorers encouraged by stories of easy wealth to the west. Not until 17 years after the conquest of Mexico, in 1520, was a real expedition sent out for exploration and conquest. Its purpose was to seek out what was to become known as the Seven Cities of Cíbola. These seven cities did not have an exact location. Old legends said they were the first home of the Aztecs, with the Aztec name of Aztlán. Aztlán was really seven great caves where the people lived. These seven caves may have been the homes of the Aztec gods, with centers of everyday life nearby. These caves, or cities, were supposed to have housed great riches. The Spanish had so far taken great wealth from the New World peoples. They had already conquered the Inca and Aztec empires and had carried away millions upon millions of dollars' worth of gold, silver, and precious jewels. The Spaniards guessed that these seven cities of Aztlán were actually the "Seven Cities of Cíbola" reported by the natives. These cities, the Spanish believed, held greater wealth than the Aztec and Inca empires combined.

Several attempts had also been made to sail ships northward along the west coast of Mexico. The ships sailed with crews whose heads were filled with wonderful tales of an island whose women were rich in pearls and gold. Other explorers looked for a shorter sailing route to the Orient, a way that would reduce the chances of scurvy, and would provide a safer, northwest passage.

Northward from Acapulco on Mexico's west coast, they had discovered what they considered to be a great island, which they named Santa Cruz. Later, the name was changed to California, from a story in the novel, *Las Sergas de Esplandián*. According to the story, " . . . on the right hand of the Indies there is an island called California very close to Terrestrial Paradise; and it was peopled by black women without any men among them, for they lived in the fashion of Amazons. . . . Their arms (weapons) were all gold and so was the harness of the wild beasts which they tamed to ride, for in the whole island there was no metal but gold." The ruler of this mythical island was said to be Queen Calafía.

One spring day in 1536, four ragged, weary men appeared at Culiacán, a frontier settlement in Nueva España. (In English, Nueva España means New Spain. The Spaniards gave this name to the lands lying northward from Panama. Today, Nueva España would include most of the countries of Central America, Mexico, and the states of southwestern United States.) These men were Alvar Nuñez Cabeza de Vaca, Alonso de Castillo Maldonado, Andrés Dorantes, and Dorantes' Black slave, Esteban. They had been members of the expedition of Pánfilo de Narváez to Florida. Narváez had sailed out in 1528 with the purpose of seeking another wealthy empire on the east coast. When the venture failed, the Narváez expedition moved westward along the Gulf Coast. Here the ships encountered a great storm. Their crews were spilled out along the coast of what is now Texas. About eighty men had survived the storm, but soon most became victims of disease or Indian capture. Cabeza de Vaca and his three companions had been among the few who had escaped drowning, only to become captive slaves of the Indians.

Later, Cabeza de Vaca told the officials at Culiacán that the four of them had gone through slavery, wanderings, and contacts with many tribes. Shortly after their capture, he had begun to make use of his medical knowledge. His herb-healing talent, combined with his clever use of psychology, gained for the Spaniards many privileges and kindnesses. Soon, his fame as a medicine man spread far. Neighboring tribes offered gifts to his captors for his services, and the other three men went along as assistant healers. Cabeza de Vaca also gained the reputation of being a generous man. The tribes respected his habit of giving away the payment for his services to those Indians in need, keeping nothing for himself. In this manner, Cabeza de Vaca had moved slowly westward in the company of his three friends and a large group of Indian followers. Many Indians began to worship the Spaniards as gods, calling them Children of the Sun.

From Cabeza de Vaca's writings, historians have attempted to trace the trail he followed from the coast of Texas to the frontier outpost of Culiacán (now the capital of the State of Sinaloa in Mexico). Most historians agree that Cabeza de Vaca eventually crossed central Texas to the Pecos River; from there he traveled to the Rio Grande somewhere west of the Big Bend and crossed it. He continued westward, probably through what is now southern New Mexico and southern Arizona into the valley of the Río Sonora in Mexico (see map). His little band then pushed south until they encountered some Spanish slave hunters from Culiacán. What a

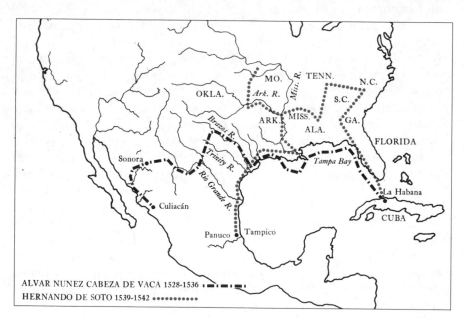

ALVAR NUNEZ CABEZA DE VACA 1528-1536 ▪━▪━▪━▪
HERNANDO DE SOTO 1539-1542 ••••••••••

meeting this must have been for both sides! The slavers from Culiacán must have been astounded to see these three heavily bearded, bronzed, nearly naked Europeans accompanied by a Black, with an escort of several hundred Indians who saw the Spaniards as the Children of the Sun. And what excitement must have stirred them when these Spaniards told of the seven great cities that existed someplace north of the path they had taken.

Everyone in Nueva España (New Spain) knew the legend about Aztlán. According to the Aztecs, the birthplace of their nation was to be found at Aztlán, which in Nahuatl, the language of the Aztec, means "place of the heron." Aztlán consisted of seven great caves to the northwest. From these caves the seven Nahua tribes (the ancestors of the Aztecs) had migrated south in the old times. Could the seven cities that Cabeza de Vaca talked about be the seven caves at Aztlán?

Antonio de Mendoza, first viceroy of Nueva España, received the four men in his study in Mexico City. He listened carefully as they recounted their experiences and told about the seven cities. They told him of the land north, far beyond the outpost of Culiacán, where lay fine cities with wealth greater than that which Cortez had found at Tenochtitlán (Mexico City). When the men left, the clever Mendoza began to think about this new information. These cities probably held hoards of emeralds, gold, and pearls. An Indian accompanying the four had been seen wearing a copper bell; that must mean the Indians of these far lands knew how to work metal. The Indians planted maize and also wore sewn skins. To wear clothing made of skins was uncommon, for the Aztecs wore clothing made of cotton.

So, beyond the northern desert was a great new land. Possibly beyond that lay a passageway connecting the two oceans. Just as important, the land was filled with "pagans" who should be taught to worship God through the Catholic religion of Spain. Viceroy Mendoza reached for paper to make plans. He would organize an expedition, using the information that Cabeza de Vaca had brought back as a basis for exploration. One of the three Spaniards could serve as a guide. Perhaps, even Esteban the Black could be the guide.

Esteban was Dorantes' slave. He had been born into slavery in Azimur on the Atlantic coast of Morocco. With Dorantes, he had shared in great adventures and what was surely the greatest walking feat in history. In Mexico City society he was again in the lowest social position, that of slave. True, he received a great deal of attention as he told over and over the story of their wanderings over the unknown northern land. But he was still a slave.

When he and his white companions had escaped their captors and made their unbelievable march westward, it had been different. He had been the one to march ahead announcing the arrival of the Children of the Sun. He had made the arrangements for the welcoming of his party. It was he more than the others who had learned the languages of the various Indian groups. It was he the Indian women had smiled at and admired. He, Esteban, had marched as the leader, beating a drum and shaking a colored feathered gourd supposedly having special powers, the gift of a medicine man. Indeed, Esteban had been known as a medicine man and a worker of magic. But in Mexico City he was merely Andrés Dorantes' slave.

More than anything else, he wanted to return to the north. He was a master of the trails and the languages. Among the Indians in the north he was an important figure. He could be a rich man; he could be free. Esteban waited for his chance.

As Esteban waited, in the short period of six years (1536–1542), seven expeditions ventured northward seeking the Seven Caves of Aztlán. Three of the expeditions were by sea, four by land.

It happened that Fray Marcos de Niza was in Mexico City for part of this period. Fray Marcos had been with Pizarro and had written of the conquest of Peru. Mendoza, anxious for success, felt that here was a man who could lead the expedition that would find the Seven Cities. When he approached the religious brother with the idea, Fray Marcos accepted most eagerly. Immediately, a group was organized with Fray Marcos, his close companion Fray Honorato, a full escort of Indians, and Esteban, who would serve the important position of interpreter and guide.

The party left in early 1539, traveling through Culiacán, where Fray Honorato dropped out because of illness. Before long, Fray Marcos began to feel a certain concern about Esteban's behavior. Esteban, making the most of his reputation as a medicine man and wizard, dressed for the part. He wore bells around his ankles and arms and carried his colorful feathered gourd rattle. Esteban was troublesome company for a man of God, Fray Marcos wrote in his journal, but if trouble with savages should come, perhaps it would be best if Esteban were to bear the weight of it. Fray Marcos ordered Esteban to travel far in advance of him, sending back a messenger when he had something to report. The messenger was to carry a small or large cross according to the importance of the finding. This plan pleased Esteban, who gathered his most faithful followers, about 300 Indians, and proceeded northward like a mighty king.

Esteban and his procession marched northward across the desert, traveling in grand style. He had with him a set of green dishes for his dinner service, and a pair of greyhounds at his heels. Fray Marcos followed days behind.

Four days after Esteban paraded into the lands closest to what is now southeastern Arizona, a messenger arrived before Fray Marcos bearing a wooden cross as tall as a man. Esteban's message was for Fray Marcos to move ahead immediately, for he had just heard about "the greatest country in the world," which was said to lie about 30 days' travel from Esteban's location. The country was called Cíbola. The messenger reported that the first part of this great country consisted of seven cities—the Seven Cities of Cíbola. (Cíbola in Zuñi language means "buffalo.")

Adventure to Cíbola

Fray Marcos could hardly believe what he heard. Could it be that he had been chosen to find the rich cities of gold and silver? He hurried forward, anxious to catch up with Esteban. Esteban did not wait as he had been ordered to do, but pressed ahead. Soon he sent back another large cross with the message that the country was even greater than he had originally been told.

As Fray Marcos traveled, he talked to Pima Indians along the way and confirmed Esteban's report. The natives said they traveled regularly to Cíbola where they traded for turquoise, hides and other goods. In reports to the viceroy, Fray Marcos made first use of the word *pueblo* to describe the towns or cities that the Indians talked about. The word eventually came into general use to describe the town-dwelling tribes of the southwestern United States.

The closer Fray Marcos got to Esteban, the more warmly the Indians received him. They looked upon the religious brother as a holy man or medicine man. But Fray Marcos had little time for converting or healing; he was eager to reach Esteban and the Seven Cities of Cíbola. Along the way he was presented with a strange "cowhide" which he reasoned could only have been cured by a highly civilized people. At this point Fray Marcos formally took possession of all these new lands for the Spanish Crown.

A third large cross arrived with the message to hurry. Fray Marcos rushed forward, trying to catch up with Esteban. For seven days he traveled through a fertile, well watered valley, probably the Yaqui River Valley in the state of Sonora in Mexico. The valley was rich in game and well populated. The Indians wore clothes made of cotton and leather and had ear pendants and necklaces of turquoise. Fray Marcos was told that the Indians of the far north wore clothes made of fabric like that of his own habit. The Indians were probably referring to the cloth the Hopi Indians made of jack-rabbit fur wound about yucca fiber.

Two days march from this valley Fray Marcos came upon a village where the people cultivated corn. These Indians repeated the stories about Cíbola. They told of streets, tall houses of many stories, and of the ladders people used to climb up to their heights.

Four days later Fray Marcos found himself in another river valley, the Sonora River Valley. He was now in the country Cabeza de Vaca had reached before heading toward Culiacán. Through this valley he journeyed five days. Time and time again he received information about Cíbola. Now he was told that there was more than one kingdom. He learned of others bearing the names of Ahacus, Marata, Totonteac, and Acus. (In reality these "towns" did exist. Ahacus was the Zuñi pueblo of Hawikuh; Marata was a group of towns which had been destroyed in warfare; Totonteac was an abandoned Hopi town in the Painted Desert of Arizona; and Acus was the fortress rock of Acoma in central New Mexico.) In this valley Fray Marcos noticed great quantities of tanned "oxhides" and of turquoise, all of which were said to come from Cíbola.

Again a message arrived from Esteban. He was now leaving the last village before his destination—Cíbola. It is now believed that he was at the village of Arispe or Bacoachi on the Sonora River and was heading towards the plains around Cananea. (See map, page 14).

Because various Indian groups along the way repeated basically the same information as Esteban's, Fray Marcos was sure the stories about Cíbola were true. He soon reached Cananea and started across the plains. For twelve days, he and his party followed what seemed to be the trail to Cíbola. The countryside offered food in the form of venison, hares, and birds of all kinds.

At this point Fray Marcos met one of Esteban's followers, exhausted and sad. The man tearfully reported that Esteban and his party had been captured by the warlike people of Hawikuh, one of the Seven Cities. This man had escaped only by chance. The news filled Fray Marcos and his party with fright. Some wanted to turn back—and yet they were so close. Fray Marcos persuaded them to continue.

They were only a day's march from Hawikuh when two Indians covered with wounds met them with the news that Esteban and his followers were dead. This time Fray Marcos could not persuade the party to push onward. However, he did manage to talk the Indian chiefs into going with him to view the place where Esteban and his followers had met their death. The three climbed a hill from where Fray Marcos could see Hawikuh. He described the view in his written reports:

> "It is situated on a level stretch on the brow of a roundish hill. It appears to be a very beautiful city, the best that I have seen in these parts. . . . The town is bigger than the city of Mexico. At times I was tempted to go to it, because I knew that I risked nothing but my life, which I had offered to God the day I commenced the journey; finally I feared to do so, considering my danger and that if I died, I would not be able to give an account of this country, which seems to me to be the greatest and best of the discoveries."

Building a large pile of stones with a cross on top, he formally laid claim to Hawikuh and the other cities of Cíbola in the names of the viceroy of Nueva España and the emperor of the Spanish Empire. He included the regions of Totonteac, Acus, and Marata and called the land the New Kingdom of Saint Francis.

This done, he hurried southward back to Culiacán, then on to Compostela where he met Governor Coronado. Here he wrote the report to be used by Coronado when in the following year he would lead his famed expedition of conquest and exploration. Little did Coronado know that the report would prove to be inaccurate and filled with fiction. No one knows why Fray Marcos wrote this false account. He had shown that he was an able mapmaker and that he understood what he observed. But the report has been called by some historians the worst geographical document ever written.

What of Esteban? Why was he killed? The answer to this question did not come until a year later when Coronado's expedition arrived in the area of Cíbola. It seems that Esteban had refused to

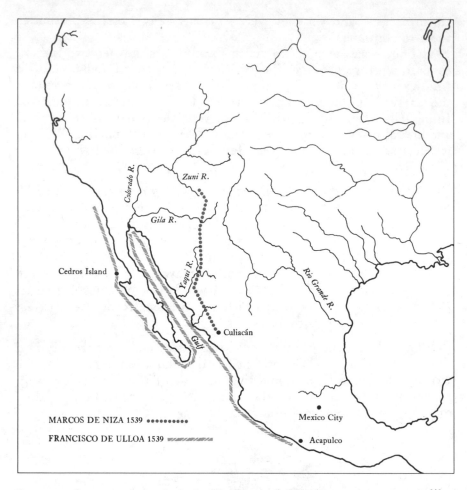

listen to the warnings that the Indians of Cíbola were more warlike
than any he had met in his travels. Esteban, as usual, had sent forward a messenger bearing his rattle gourd. But the white and red
feathers that decorated this symbol of power did not possess the
same magic that it had for other Indians. Instead, the Indians of
the pueblo recognized it as the sign of a tribe with which they had
been at war for a long time. The chiefs of Cíbola warned Esteban
not to enter. But Esteban would not listen. He felt that once the
people of Cíbola saw him all would be well; so he marched in
proudly with tinkling bells. Esteban then demanded that everyone
listen to him. He said that he had come ahead to make preparations
for a white man, the representative of a great lord. The chiefs,
though, could not understand why a white man would have sent a
black messenger. They felt that he must be the spy for black invaders from the south. Furthermore, Esteban made greedy de-

mands. He asked for turquoise and great amounts of food. He even made advances to some of the women. The chiefs, angered and suspicious, refused to give anything. The next morning Esteban and some of his followers left their campsite to explore. Watchful people of the pueblo, fearing that the black stranger was attempting to escape, ran for him. Esteban and his followers fled. The people of Cíbola shot their arrows. Esteban fell dead, his dreams of wealth and freedom unfulfilled.

The chiefs cut up Esteban's body and sent portions of it to all the chiefs of the seven pueblos. To the chief lord of all the cities went the greatest prize, the two greyhounds and the four green dinner plates.

To this day the people of Zuñi tell in their tales of a black man with two huge dogs who came among them to do them evil.

PART II — THE CONQUEST OF CÍBOLA

Other Expeditions

The greatest and most exciting expedition, inspired by the reports of Cabeza de Vaca and Fray Marcos would be that of Coronado. But there were others, some famous, others less well known. Among the lesser ventures was the Francisco de Ulloa expedition.

Ulloa had sailed north from Acapulco in July 1539, hoping to reach the Seven Cities by sea. He did not succeed, of course. He did prove, though, that California was not the mythical island ruled by Queen Calafía but was actually an extension of the mainland, partly a peninsula. Ulloa's party had sailed north to the head of the Gulf of California where they attempted to enter the Colorado River. They had to give up the attempt, however, because the violent waters at the river's mouth almost caused the ships to overturn. Ulloa then returned southward to the tip of Lower California and sailed up the Pacific side to Cedros Island, where they put in for the winter months. In April 1540, one ship was sent back to Acapulco with the news that Ulloa was continuing to sail up the Pacific coast. This was the last that was ever heard from him or his men. In all likelihood, they were dashed to pieces on the rocky coast of California.

In the same year, two other men were stirred into action, Hernando de Soto and Pedro de Alvarado. When Hernando de Soto heard of Cabeza de Vaca's journey, he got official approval to conquer the land north of Cuba. De Soto and his men landed near Tampa Bay on the west coast of Florida, where they found Juan Ortiz, a survivor of the Narváez expedition in which Cabeza de

Vaca, Esteban, and the others had figured. Juan Ortiz had been living among the Indians for ten years and had heard that gold was
to be found somewhere inland to the north. Using Ortiz as guide
and interpreter, de Soto and his men began a march which lasted
for three years. They crossed what today are Georgia, South
Carolina, North Carolina, Tennessee, Alabama, and Mississippi.
They passed over the great river and wandered through Arkansas,
coming at one time to within 300 miles of the Coronado expedition.
Perhaps had the two expeditions met, the course of history would
have been changed.

No gold was ever found by de Soto. When Juan Ortiz died, the
explorer was left without guide or interpreter. Because he was ill,
de Soto decided to head back, following the Mississippi River
south. Too ill to survive the trip, he died in July 1542. Because his
men wanted to keep the Indians believing the myth that white men
were immortal, they buried de Soto in the waters of the Mississippi
and told the Indians he had gone for a visit to heaven.

Luis de Moscoso was elected as the new leader to take the
expedition back to the coast. Their first attempt was an overland
route westward which led them into present-day Texas. Here they
found out about Coronado's expedition and also picked up evidence
that Cabeza de Vaca had traveled through this area. Short of
food, the expedition returned to the river where they built seven
small boats. After suffering many attacks from Indians, they
reached the sea. Enduring a terrible voyage along the Texas coast,
they finally arrived at the Spanish settlement at Panuco (Tampico).
The 300 survivors had nothing to show for their three years of
wandering. They did, however, have much to report about the land
northward.

The second expedition was led by Pedro de Alvarado. Its
mission was to conquer the Spice Islands. But when Alvarado heard
of the findings of Fray Marcos he asked for the right to follow up
these discoveries, using his own fleet of ships. The officials told him
to remember his orders to conquer the Spice Islands. So it was that

the expedition of Alvarado sailed up the Mexican coast as far as Santiago.

In 1539, Viceroy Mendoza launched his plan for the conquest of the Seven Cities of Cíbola. He ordered the *alcalde* (mayor) of Culiacán, Melchor Díaz, to gather careful information about the route traveled by Fray Marcos, and he requested that Hernando de Alarcón command three supply ships. These ships were to sail up the Gulf of California and offer support to the main expedition, which was to follow the overland route.

The overland expedition was put under the command of Francisco Vásquez de Coronado, a young nobleman who was a favorite of Mendoza's. Coronado had just been made governor of *Nueva Galicia,* the northernmost province of Nueva España.

Adventure-seeking *caballeros* (gentleman soldiers) lost no time in volunteering for the Coronado expedition. As it was they were bored and were loafing about creating mischief. They wanted fortune and adventure and were anxious to be off in search of the fabulous cities in the far north. The *caballeros* had missed out on the other expeditions that had recently left Nueva España. Mendoza was as delighted to be rid of them as he was eager to launch the expedition.

At Compostela on February 22, 1540, the army started its journey to Culiacán, the jumping-off city for the north—and the riches of Cíbola. This army of conquest has been described as being one of the most distinguished and noble ever to gather in the "Indies." At the head of the company, surrounded by his lieutenants and Fray Marcos, rode Coronado in gilded armor. Throughout the adventures that armor was to serve as an attraction for many hard blows. Behind Coronado rode 225 skilled horsemen, *caballeros,* all mounted on the finest horseflesh that Nueva España and Spain could breed. Most of the *caballeros* wore armor made of buckskin; the Spanish had learned in the conquest of the Aztecs that leather was as effective as metal armor against the Indian weapons. Behind the *caballeros* marched 60 foot-soldiers armed with pikes, crossbows, and harquebuses (clumsy firearms). Following the foot-soldiers, a rather disorderly crowd of Indian servants and Black slaves drove the baggage animals and pulled the six *pedreros,* light field pieces of bronze. Bringing up the rear in grand style were 1,000 Indian allies in full war regalia of colorful feathered headdresses and warpaint, carrying bows, slings and flint-edged maces. It is interesting to note that only one Spanish woman accompanied the expedition, Señora María Maldonado de Paladinas, wife of the storekeeper.

Certainly more important than the details of this army bent on the conquest and exploration of Cíbola is the understanding of the general character of the peoples involved.

The Spanish *caballero* was much like a knight from the Middle Ages. Like the knight, the *caballero* was first of all a soldier. As such, he was used to hardship and was willing to take on all that went with war. But he would have nothing to do with physical labor. In his mind, such low work was fitting only for slaves and servants. Most commonly, the *caballeros* had come to the New World seeking fame and fortune. They believed that wealth was acquired by inheritance, gambling, or prizes. The *caballero* generally looked upon himself as champion of the Catholic Church, although he was a defender of its power more than its teachings. He was proud of being white and of being Spanish and often held the Indian in contempt. Physically, he was tough, athletic, and used to carrying the burden of armor.

His opponent was the red man, the Indian. In contrast, his way of life was based on varied backgrounds and origins. The Indians came from many tribes whose homelands extended from the Nayarít swamp to the Missouri basin. The tribal names included the Huichol, Cora, Totoram, Tepihuan, Tahu, Guasave, Xixime, Acaxee, Coheta, Yaqui, Mayo, Pima, Cocopa, Yuma, Zuñi, Hopi, Tehua, Tigrea, Queres, Piro, Apache, Caddo, Wichita, Pawnee. Among these various groups, different levels of development existed. Some were well-organized, strong, and able to stand off the white invaders. Others were not. Like the invaders, most were daring, and capable of withstanding great hardships. As fighters they were clever and able to act quickly and to battle with determination. As warriors, they were a match for the Spaniards in discipline and fierceness. However, in one important aspect they were weaker. Most Indians were still living in a Stone Age culture. They owned no large domesticated animals which they could ride or work. Their agricultural tools were crude; they had not yet realized the use of the wheel. The northernmost tribes had learned to work some metal, but had developed no weapons that could equal the firearms of the Spaniards. In all, they had little of what the Spaniards would consider necessary to classify them as "civilized" people.

However, the limitations of the Indian people were unknown to the Spaniards when on February 22, 1540, they launched their invasion. This great expedition was motivated by two forces: gold and God. The land before them was said to be rich with the metal that brought fame and fortune—and full of souls who should be gathered into the great flock of Mother Church.

At first, progress was slow. The 558 horses were overloaded with baggage, much of it useless. The conquerors were newcomers to this kind of warfare, with little understanding of the land. Their trail was clearly marked by the fancy heavy equipment they discarded along the way. There was no planned conservation of materials. Each man was responsible for his own uniform and food, and, if he rode a horse, for his mount.

Bringing up the rear of the column were large herds of cattle, sheep and swine—food on the hoof. These animals could scarcely be forced to keep up with the desired pace of the conquerors, and they created delays and other problems at every crossing of river or swamp. Furthermore, the 1,000 Indians who accompanied the army were of little help, for they had to be treated as allies, not servants. Thus, this grand army of *conquistadores* (conquerors) was able to travel a total distance of 185 miles in about 20 days.

Along the way the expedition was joined by the reconnaissance party of Melchor Díaz, who warned them of the rugged, barren land ahead that threatened difficulty for Coronado's huge army. Coronado, however, gave little thought to his advice.

In July, after following the trail that Fray Marcos indicated, the advance group reached Hawikuh. It was the first of the Zuñi pueblos and the same one that had resisted Esteban's intrusion. This "golden city" turned out to be a small village on the shores of the Zuñi River, or Río Vermejo. (See map, page 21.) As Coronado and his men drew closer it became clear that this was hardly a city of gold. What a disappointment the first view of this simple village must have been! On what kind of fool's journey had Fray Marcos led them? So great was their anger against him that he took the first opportunity to return to the safety of Mexico City.

Coronado fully expected that the inhabitants of Hawikuh would bow low before him in fear and awe. But the Zuñis showed no such submission. Instead, they gave every indication that they would defend their pueblo. Unlike most Indians of the Americas, they were not frightened by their first sight of horses. They were used to seeing huge beasts, for they were familiar with buffalo and elk. They met the demands for surrender with angry shouts and a flight of arrows.

At first Coronado held back, hoping to convince the Zuñis that they would be wise to accept Spanish rule. When he realized that the Zuñis meant to resist, he gave the ancient Spanish battle cry, *"Cierra, España y Santiago!"* ("Fight for Spain and St. James!"), and charged. The Indians prepared for battle. Retreating to the inside of their buildings, they lined the terraces, firing arrows and slinging stones at the Spaniards. The fight raged. Several Indians were killed, a few Spaniards were injured, and three horses were fatally wounded. Coronado himself received the severest wound among the Spaniards, probably because his splendid armor set him off as a prize target. Oddly, the Indian allies were not allowed to take part in the battle.

The Hawikuh warriors' resistance weakened as their supply of rocks and arrows dwindled. As they drew back from their village the Spaniards moved in fast, grabbing all food supplies. At this point in the conquest, after some six months in the field, the possession of food was more valuable to them than treasure chests of gold. The conquerors had almost exhausted their own supply.

It did not take long for Coronado and his men to complete the conquest of the remaining Seven Cities or, rather, the Zuñi pueblos. While they found no gold, emeralds or pearls, they did at least capture supplies of corn and beans.

Coronado and his men had no choice but to continue exploring and conquering. Pedro de Tovar and Fray Juan de Padilla were sent westward with a small company. They met the Hopi tribe and took them over with little effort. No fighting was involved for the Hopi people simply handed themselves over to the Spaniards. In the Hopi language, their name *Hopitu* means "the peaceful ones." (Later, history changed the "peaceful ones" into warriors. They bravely regained their freedom and stubbornly held onto it, giving in only when the Anglo American took over the Southwest.) In the "conquest" of the Hopi pueblos, the Spaniards learned of the existence of a great river farther west.

A second group under the command of Melchor Díaz was sent back along the trail to establish a base on the Sonora River. From there, the group was to work its way westward and meet the three supply ships under Alarcón's command. Díaz's company managed to reach the Colorado River, only to find that Alarcón had sailed away three days earlier after growing tired of waiting. Although he left a letter in the expectation that Coronado's expedition would reach the spot, Alarcón deposited neither boats nor supplies. Nevertheless, Díaz continued his mission westward, crossing into what is now California. One day he was seriously injured in a hunting accident, and the company was forced to turn back, carrying the fatally

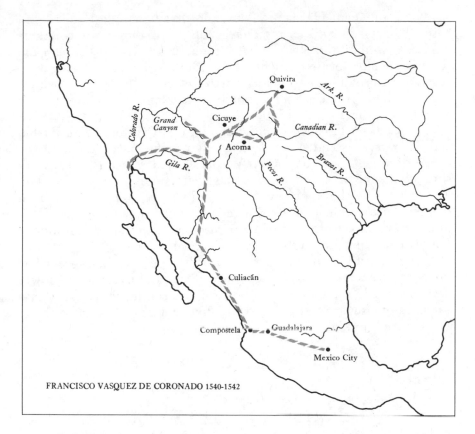

FRANCISCO VASQUEZ DE CORONADO 1540-1542

wounded man for twenty days before he died. Had Díaz and his party been able to continue their march, they might have reached the Pacific, thus proving that the Pacific Ocean could be reached by an overland trail.

Meantime, Tovar returned to Coronado and reported his victory over the Hopi. He also repeated Indian accounts of a "great river to the west." Coronado immediately sent García Lopez de Cárdenas in search of the river. After twenty days, Lopez de Cárdenas found what he called "el Gran Cañon del Río Colorado," becoming the "discoverer" of one of the world's great natural wonders, the Grand Canyon.

Coronado judged from the reports of Tovar and Lopez de Cárdenas that to explore to the west in great force would be unproductive. Instead, he thought it better to direct his attention eastward where, according to the Indians, there existed another great pueblo, Acoma the Holy City. While he weighed the choice, two chiefs from the distant Pecos pueblos came seeking friendship with the white strangers. Coronado responded to their request by sending Lieutenant Hernando Alvarado, Fray Juan de Padilla, and a small party of *caballeros*. The group, with the Pecos chiefs as guides, passed by the Sky City of Acoma and traveled through the Tigeux pueblos located on the Rio Grande near the present community of Bernalillo. Continuing north through other small pueblos, they reached Braba (Taos), finally returning by way of Cicuye (Pecos) in the fall of 1540.

In each pueblo they found a similarity of culture. The Pueblo Indians were descendants of cliff dwellers who once inhabited the caves of huge rocks at Mesa Verde, Chaco Canyon, and areas throughout the present Southwest, as well as northern Mexico. Unlike the cliff dwellers, however, they built their houses in the open desert. The Pueblo house consisted of many square rooms. Each house was joined to the next, like rows of building blocks. Adjoining houses had common roofs or walls. The buildings were generally two or three stories high, with some rising five and six stories. The upper stories were set back, like stairs. Thus, the roofs of the lower stories served as floors or balconies for the rooms above. It is easy to see how several families could live comfortably in such an "apartment building."

The materials used for these buildings were mainly adobe and wood. To make adobe, a shallow pit is dug in clay soil. The builder crumbles up some earth into it and adds water, mixing the mud into a sticky paste. From time to time he presses in layers of thin grass or straw to keep the adobe from cracking while it dries.

The wood formed the framework for the building, along which the adobe walls were shaped. The roof rested on pine *vigas* (beams) laid across the half-dried walls. These walls were extremely thick (sometimes two feet or more) and the spaces between them were as wide as the shortest crossbeam. The resulting structure was strong and cool and was well able to support additional stories.

The lower story of the Pueblo house had no doors or windows to break the unity of the outer walls. The Pueblos entered their apartments by an outdoor ladder. These ladders were tree trunks with the lopped-off ends of branches serving as footholds. The ladders could be quickly pulled up when the pueblo was in danger.

Within the apartment, people could go down to the first story, a sort of supply room, by way of an inside ladder through a hole in the roof.

The Pueblos had developed a life style different from that of all the other tribes in the northern lands of Nueva España. They were no longer nomadic hunters who followed the wild herds. They had settled and now depended on the soil for their living. Their agricultural life had led them to build permanent homes and to develop a village type of society. Because they had learned how to store food, they had enough free time and comfort to create works of art and a complex form of worship.

Each pueblo was arranged as an independent republic ruled by a council of elders. The Spaniards were able to identify some of these elders as priests, who would preach to the people from their position on the highest terrace.

The Spaniards were surprised at the lack of crime within the pueblo. The explanation was that very little property was held by individuals. Most of it, especially the land, was kept by the entire community.

The Pueblo Indians were able fighters, more defensive than offensive, in sharp contrast to their neighbors and enemies, the Apaches. Occasionally there were battles, but by nature the Pueblos preferred to live in isolation and peace. Sometimes the Pueblos would organize into an alliance to meet a particular problem, with the organization lasting only until the common danger had passed. The people of the pueblos did not trade back and forth except for turquoise, which they all held sacred. Indeed, they kept so much to themselves that in some cases Indians from different pueblos could communicate only in sign language. Sign language, in fact, served as the common communication among the various tribes that Coronado met.

Like all Indians of the New World, the Pueblos worshiped the elements of nature. They believed that the Sun was the creator of life, and in all their religious ceremonies the Sun played the lead role. One artistic aspect of these ceremonies was the dance. Dances were dedicated to the sun, the rain, or the growth of corn. Preceded by ceremonial sand painting, the dances were accompanied by drum and flute and performed in costumes and masks. To this day, they are colorful and exciting to watch.

In other artistic expressions the Pueblos made pottery and baskets as well as blankets, decorating their handwork with religious symbols. The even shape of their pottery was the result of highly skilled handling, for they did not know the potter's wheel. The high degree of their artistry indicated the great amounts of time spent in the working of an object. Time itself had no value to them. Unlike the Indians of central and southern Mexico, the Pueblos had not developed a calendar.

Their attitude towards time allowed the Pueblos to develop complex ceremonies around many aspects of their lives. Even the hunt, whether of lion, bear, deer, buffalo, turkey or rabbit, required a special ceremony. Fish was never eaten, for it was considered to be sacred.

Water was of great significance to the desert Indian. In this arid and dusty land, settlement was possible only along thin, living streams. The Pueblos' greatest dances were those which begged the great spirit for life-giving showers. The coming of rain made possible the cultivation of corn, pumpkins and beans, providing them with food to store away against the greatly feared periods of drought. The Pueblos understood irrigation and used it. They also stored water in cisterns, large hollow places in the rocks.

Town sites were picked on the basis of how easily the Pueblos could get water and how well the spot could be defended. Most pueblos were built a good distance from hunting grounds. Great importance was placed on security, even if it meant that the people had to travel great distances to secure timber and food. The houses of the pueblos were constructed with thick walls in order to withstand attack, a further indication of the Pueblos' concern for safety from their enemies. What the Pueblo people dreaded was the roving hunters. They had good reason to fear attack. The nomadic Navajos, Utes, Apaches, and Comanches were not in the habit of storing food. Their way, the way of the hunter, was to pursue the herds across the plains or to track game through the forests. When conditions were not favorable the hunters could not follow their familiar ways. Sometimes, for instance, war took every man from the hunt. At times, drought forced the game animals to wander far away. Then it was that the hunters crossed the desert to the pueblos. There they would raid the stored food supplies and carry them back to the hungry tribes. These nomads needed fruit and vegetables as well as meat in their diet. Like sailors, nomadic Indians often suffered from scurvy, a very disagreeable illness which results from lack of Vitamin C. During the dry season, the grasslands and forests yielded few natural sources of Vitamin C in the form of wild fruits and vegetables.

The heart of each pueblo was the *kiva,* the Hopi name for the chamber which the Spaniards called *estufa,* meaning stove. Only men were allowed into the *kiva,* which served as a clubroom, a school for boys, a lodge hall for a male secret society, and a place of worship.

All aspects of the pueblo were a response to the natural environment that so controlled the Indians' lives. The dress of the Pueblos showed such a response. Men wore short tunics, trousers, leggings, and moccasins, all made of deerskin, topped with a decorated skin cap. In winter they wore robes of yucca fiber woven with rabbit skin or mountain lion skin. For special days they had cloaks of feathers or blankets made of woven cotton. Men cut their hair in bangs and braided the rest, tying back the braids with a headband. Women wore a woven skirt covered by a blanket-like garment that draped over the right shoulder and under the left arm, fastened at the waist by a wide belt or sash. They wore leggings and moccasins as the men did. Their hair was usually parted in the middle and braided. Young girls who had reached the marriageable age wore disc-shaped puffs on each side of their heads. Men as well as women decorated themselves with the sacred turquoise and ornaments made of drilled shell, and for ceremonies and tribal dances they painted their bodies.

It is important to understand that the Spanish contribution to the "civilizing" of the Pueblos was limited. These Indians had learned to live sensibly and comfortably with their environment. Where they could not control outside forces they looked to a power greater than themselves for help. In exchange for the Spaniards' introduction to these people of a variety of domestic animals, the Indian gave to the white man a knowledge of how to work the land's resources and how to adapt to its characteristics. To this day the architectural style of the Pueblos is clearly evident in most communities throughout the Southwest. Many Indian people, like their architecture, have survived the centuries practically unchanged. The culture of the Pueblos continues today much as it was in 1540, when Coronado first "conquered" it.

While at Pecos, Lieutenant Alvarado became keenly interested in two captives held by the Indians as slaves. One of them was a Pawnee whom the Spaniards called "El Turco" because of his headdress. The other was a Wichita, named Isopete. Alvarado was allowed to take the men when he left. They led Alvarado and his men into the high plains at the head of the Canadian River. From there they pointed out the great herds of buffalo. For the Spaniards, it was the first sight of these massive "cows" or "hump-backed oxen" as Cabeza de Vaca had labeled them. One Spaniard described them as follows:

> "They have a narrow, short face, the brow two spans across from eye to eye, the eye sticking out at the side so that, when they are running, they can see who is following them. They have very long beards, like goats, and when they are running they throw their heads back with the beard dragging on the ground. From the middle of the body rearwards, they have tapering waists. The hair is very woolly, like a sheep's, very fine and, in front of the girdle, the hair is very long and rough like a lion's. The horns are short and thick, so that they are not visible much above the hair. In May, they change the hair in the middle of the body for a soft pelt, which makes perfect lions of them. They rub against the small trees in the little ravines to shed their hair, and they continue this until only the fuzz is left, as a snake changes its skin. They have a short tail with a bunch of hair at the end. When they run, they carry it erect like a scorpion. It is worth noting that the little calves are red, and just like ours, but they change their color and appearance with time and age." [1]

As they continued their march, the *conquistadores* came across still more buffalo each day until they were almost lost in a sea of the great animals. They killed a few but could not stay to enjoy the hunt, for Alvarado was anxious to rejoin Coronado. He was excited by El Turco's many remarks about Quivira, a city lying eastward which held great treasure of gold and silver.

When Alvarado rejoined Coronado at Tiguex, he found that winter quarters had been set up. The preparation had not involved the building of new dwellings; it had been simpler to empty one of the Tiguex pueblos of its inhabitants and move in. This pueblo, Alcanfor (cedar), was well located on the Rio Grande with a fine view of the Sandia Mountains and the broad valley below.

Lieutenant Alvarado returned to an unhappy situation. The Tiguex people had become hostile. The Spanish takeover of blankets, houses and Indian women had caused anger and bitterness. Open warfare broke out and lasted most of that winter. In the end, most of the twelve Tiguex villages were destroyed and their inhabitants killed.

With the coming of spring, Coronado marched eastward to find Quivira with El Turco and Isopete as guides. The great army of

---

[1] *Coronado's Quest,* A. Grove Day, University of California Press, 1964, pp. 228–230.

1500 marched past many camps of nomadic Indians into the *Llano Estacado* (Staked Plain). Traveling across the plains was an experience far beyond the imaginations of the Spaniards. The vastness of that flat, empty land led Coronado to write: ". . . not a stone, not a bit of rising ground, not a tree, not a shrub, nor anything to go by. . . ." One of the disbelieving *caballeros* recorded the following:

"Who could believe that a thousand horses and five hundred of our cows, and more than 5000 rams and ewes, and more than 1500 friendly Indians and servants in traveling over those plains, would leave no more trace when they had passed

than if nothing had been there—nothing—so that it was necessary to make piles of bones and cow dung now and then, so that the rear guard could follow the army. . . . Like the inside of a bowl, so that wherever a man stands, the sky hems in at a bow's shot's distance away." [2]

Eventually, they found themselves among Indians who spoke to them about *Tejas* (in the language of the Indians, "friends, allies"), and told them that the land toward which they were heading was barren and forbidding. At this point, the two guides broke down and confessed that they had been leading the Spaniards not to Quivira, but to *Tejas* (Texas). The people of the Tiguex pueblos had promised El Turco and Isopete their freedom if they would guide the Spaniards to certain death on the arid plains. The two guides were slapped into irons. The army changed direction, now moving northward. After some days they actually came to Quivira, which turned out to be a collection of poor villages located near present-day Lyons, Kansas.

Now Coronado realized that further exploration would yield them no gold, no form of treasure at all. To make matters worse, Isopete warned Coronado of more danger. El Turco was plotting with the Wichitas to lay an ambush against the army and destroy all of them. For this additional treachery El Turco paid with his life.

[2] *Op cit*, pp. 229–30.

At this point the weary Coronado expedition was encamped not far from the de Soto party, for de Soto was then exploring the Arkansas River. Had the two forces met, they might have established a permanent Spanish settlement. At worst, they might have battled for the right to search farther for the treasure that had escaped them both.

From Tiguex the disappointed and exhausted army trudged on, taking a more direct route to the headwaters of the Canadian River and across the Pecos foothills to face a second winter encampment. Their situation became worse when Coronado, while riding with his officers, fell from his loosened saddle and severely injured his head. He lay at the point of death for weeks, finally recovering enough to lead his army out of winter quarters and into Nueva España. The moment of the Spaniards' parting with the Indians was in many cases tearful and heartbreaking. Many of the Pueblo women had developed close relationships with the men, these Children of the Sun.

Almost all of the party returned to Nueva España. Three religious brothers and their servants, however, felt a greater calling to serve God than to seek for gold. These men chose to remain in the "pagan" land to try to convert the Pueblos to the "true" faith. Luis de Escalonas went to Pecos; Juan de Padilla went to Quivira; Juan de la Cruz stayed at Tiguex. In time, all three became martyrs (people who are willing to die for their beliefs). However, Andrés de Campo, who had accompanied Juan de Padilla to Quivira, somehow escaped martyrdom. He completed a journey that rivaled that of Cabeza de Vaca. De Campo wandered southward over plains and deserts, crossed the Rio Grande and struggled over the mountains to the port of Panuco, finally reaching Mexico City a full five years after the Coronado expedition.

Coronado returned to Mexico City without treasure or anything of value that could be used to pay off the huge cost for the splendid quest of the Seven Cities. To Viceroy Mendoza, Coronado's failure was an embarrassment for which he must answer to the king. To the men of the expedition, it meant being left with no more than a purseful of empty dreams. To Coronado himself, it meant the heavy bitter feeling of defeat. He returned to his post as governor of Nueva Galicia, but only for a short while. Soon he had to face charges brought against him by disappointed and unhappy men from the expedition. Any relief he gained by being found not guilty was only temporary, for he was brought up on other charges, found guilty, and imprisoned. Not only did he lose most of his personal wealth; he was also exiled to a small island in the

Mediterranean, where he served in a very minor government position.

While Coronado never found great riches on the northern frontier of Nueva España, he did determine the true extent of the North American continent. He provided detailed information concerning the land and its inhabitants, making possible future colonization. In addition, Coronado and his men exchanged with the peoples of the Southwest the seeds of Spanish and Mexican Indian cultures. The evidence of this cultural exchange appeared almost immediately in daily living. It worked a change in food and in the use of natural resources. It caused an adaptation of forms of clothing, tools, and artifacts. Probably the most important change of all was to be found in language.

2
Gold and God

PART I—THE CONTINUING SEARCH

Expansion of the Northern Frontier

The period of exploration and conquest of Aztlán, or the northern frontier of Nueva España, was not finished. Yet the activity that followed did not carry the same energy and spirit as had the search for the Seven Cities of Cíbola. The reasons are not hard to understand. Within any exploratory movement must come periods for thinking things over, analyzing what has happened, figuring out how to move ahead in the best way. During such times, people realize that their plans have not come out exactly as they originally intended. In a way this process follows almost every venture into the unknown. A country goes through it; a team of scientists goes through it; even a child goes through it with a new puzzle. Ventures into the unknown may be called failures in terms of their not achieving original goals. But history shows over and over that what is gathered in terms of other knowledge is often more important.

During this second period of exploration much of what took place was based on information brought back by the Coronado

expedition. As Cabeza de Vaca had filled Coronado with the desire
to investigate new lands, so Coronado was to inspire many others
with that restless interest to explore. Coronado's failure to repeat
the success of Cortez in finding immense wealth did not kill the
dream of riches in Aztlán. The northward movement into the unknown went ahead, but at a slower pace. People realized that the
land would indeed yield riches—but not without hard work.

For the ambitious, the tight controls of the Spanish Crown
were discouraging. Virtually all enterprises were taken over in the
Crown's name. The few areas left open for free development were
the frontiers of the north. These northern areas, therefore, became
the places where new enterprises appeared—cattle and sheep ranching, and an occasional bonanza in mining.

The northern frontier was a magnet attracting adventurers
seeking easy money; settlers hoping to plant roots for future generations; dreamers and creators wishing to escape the control of
authorities; missionaries seeking outlets for their strong dedication;
and endless others who for many and mixed reasons pushed to the
frontier.

At the same time, the Crown was determined to maintain its
authority. It held strict control over its peoples, demanding from
each *la quinta* (one-fifth of whatever was gained). The Crown was
always looking for ways to replenish the royal treasury. Thus, the
Spanish Crown supported new ideas and schemes that would en-
hance its *quinta*. Among these new ventures was the Manila Galleon
fleet, which directly affected the northward expansion into the
Southwest.

The Manila Galleon fleet consisted of ships that sailed westward, aided by the trade winds, from Acapulco to the Philippines
and the Orient. From the Spanish port of Manila, in the Philippines,
the fleet gained its name. They returned by way of the Japanese
and northern Pacific currents to the coast of California; from the
coast they would sail southward back to Acapulco. These great
sailing vessels were well armed and constructed with huge holds to
carry their cargoes. Generally, the ships sailed out with gold from
the mines of Mexico and some marketable goods from Spain as

well as Mexico. They returned loaded with spices, silks, porcelains, woods, and exotic items of an almost unbelievable variety for the markets of Spain and the colonies of the New World. One account tells of cargoes of thousands of women's combs, fans, bric-a-brac of ivory, jade and jasper, brass toothpicks, finely carved and inlaid boxes, "drugs" such as musk, borax, and camphor, tea, fine cotton, embroideries, Persian rugs and carpets, and, in one case, more than 50,000 pairs of silk stockings in just one cargo.

This trade with the Orient had begun with the continued attempts to find a navigable passageway from Europe to Asia, the mythical "Strait of Anian." To seek this passageway, the Spanish Crown had invested in a series of operations. One of these was a voyage commanded by the Portuguese sailor, Juan Rodriguez Cabrillo.

In 1542, Cabrillo sailed with two ships northward from Puerto de Navidad on the Pacific Coast. At one point they made contact with some Indians who spoke of seeking men who looked like Cabrillo and his crew about five days' journey inland, probably meaning the Díaz group from the Coronado expedition. Cabrillo attempted to contact the other white men but failed. Struggling farther north against strong currents, the ships reached the island of San Miguel where the crew spent the winter. Cabrillo did not survive the winter and died there January 3, 1543.

Command of the ships was taken over by the pilot, Bartolomé Ferrer, who directed the expedition to set sail again the following month. On March 1, they marked the site of the mouth of a great river, at about 42° north latitude (the Rogue River in Oregon). This was the northernmost point they reached, for the weather was heavy and the food scarce. The return voyage was rough, forcing the ships to lose one another for a time. They finally made Puerto de Navidad in April 1543. Once again, no great discovery had been made. Yet these men in their tiny ships had traveled over 800 miles through some of the most dangerous of sea routes. Furthermore, the voyage added proof of the vastness of the North American continent.

The Cabrillo-Ferrelo expedition was followed by many more but with a different emphasis: the establishment of routes between Nueva España and the Orient.

In 1545, Ruy Lopez de Villalobos crossed the Pacific Ocean from Nueva España to San Lázaro, where he claimed and renamed the Philippine Islands for his emperor, Philip III. In 1565, 20 years later, Miguel Lopez de Legazpi led another voyage from Nueva España to the Philippines, which were then placed under the control of the viceroy of Nueva España. So began the very rich trade

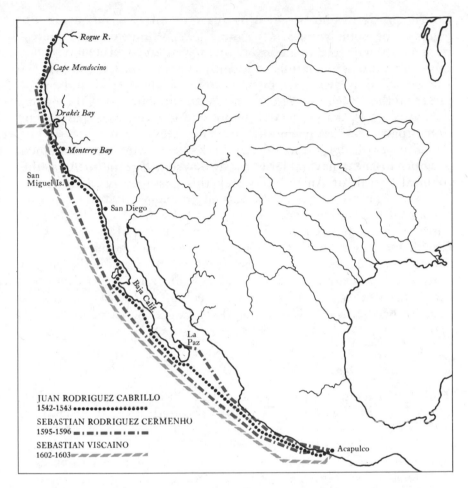

JUAN RODRIGUEZ CABRILLO
1542-1543 ●●●●●●●●●●●●●●●

SEBASTIAN RODRIGUEZ CERMENHO
1595-1596 ▬ ▪ ▬ ▪ ▬ ▪ ▬ ▪ ▬

SEBASTIAN VISCAINO
1602-1603 ▬ ▬ ▬ ▬ ▬ ▬ ◢

between Nueva España and the Orient by means of the Manila Galleons.

With the establishment of trans-Pacific trade, California took on special importance for Spain, for the Manila Galleons needed that coast. The news came that the Englishman, Sir Francis Drake, in his circumnavigation of the world, had put in along the coast of California, north of present-day San Francisco (Drake's Bay) and claimed the land in the name of the English Crown. Another Englishman, Thomas Cavendish, raided the coasts of Peru and Nueva España in 1587. He even captured one of the Manila Galleons off the coast of California.

Filled with fear of the English threat, the viceroy of Nueva España immediately sent out one of the *capitanes* (captains) of the Manila fleet to scout the coast of California to determine the best way to defend it. The captain, a Portuguese named Sebastian

Rodriguez Cermenho, stopped on his return trip from the Philippines at the point known as Drake's Bay. While his crew built a launch to navigate the shallow waters, Captain Cermenho slowly began to make his analysis. Suddenly a storm arose, sinking the treasure-filled galleon. Cermenho and his crew were forced to return to the mother port in the small launch. In spite of the loss of the galleon and its wealth, Cermenho had gained a great deal. The slow progress of the launch had made possible the careful and exact observation of the coast. The notes collected by the crew later proved most important in the settlement of the California coast colonies.

Even before Cermenho returned to Nueva España, another captain of the Manila fleet was on his way to California. Sebastian Viscaino had obtained permission to conquer and colonize California. He was allowed to engage also in the rich business of pearl fishing. Viscaino, as part of his contract, was to provide the viceroy with detailed information about the California coast. Viscaino outfitted three ships and recruited some colonists. He also convinced four Franciscan brothers to come along to give spiritual help to his project.

Efforts to Colonize

The first attempt at colonization was made at the tip of Baja California, at La Paz. Viscaino deposited his little band of colonists there and continued northward along the Pacific coast. The stormy conditions of the winter of 1596, like those which discouraged the Ferrelo expedition, drove back Viscaino's ships. The weather had also disheartened the colonists of La Paz. The returning ships mercifully brought back the sick and starving colonists to Nueva España. Viscaino, however, did not abandon his plans. In 1602 he organized a second expedition and once more sailed north to California.

This expedition, consisting of three ships, left Acapulco in May. In November they entered a harbor which they named San Diego. Continuing northward, they sailed into Monterey Bay, which Viscaino described as being well-sheltered, well-inhabited, and surrounded by fertile land. By January 1603, they reached Cape Mendocino. Here the combination of cold weather, lack of food, and a sickly crew forced the expedition to return to Acapulco. Viscaino's reports, especially about Monterey Bay, inspired many people to plan for a pioneer colony there. But the viceroy was not convinced that such an undertaking would be practical. Partly as a result, California remained uncolonized for another 160 years.

While these events were taking place on the west coast of Mexico, a great mine of silver was opened in central Nueva España. The mines of Zacatecas earned their discoverers and the Crown a long-range source of capital. The mines also acted as a magnet, attracting people and goods developed for the new community. From Zacatecas a movement slowly pushed out toward the friendlier regions of an otherwise arid and barren land. By 1585 Santa Barbara (in the State of Chihuahua) on the Rio Conchos and Monterey (in the State of Nuevo Leon) had been established as the northernmost communities of Nueva España.

The discovery of silver mines, rich beyond belief, erased some of the disappointment that had followed Coronado's failure to find treasure in the far north. The interest in Cíbola did not revive until the frontier settlements edged closer to the region of the Seven Cities.

A new route down the Rio Conchos to the Rio del Norte (Rio Grande) avoided the long dangerous crossing of the deserts and plains north of Culiacán. Once again small parties probed northward, this time to find out whether pueblos rumored to lie in that direction were the same ones Coronado had found. Missionaries soon followed their paths, while others traveled as far as the great plains to the northeast.

One Franciscan lay brother, Fray Agustín Rodriguez, led a missionary group to the Tiguex pueblos. He did not know that Coronado's army had stayed there some forty years previously. The people of these pueblos, however, remembered all too clearly their unhappy encounter with the white men. They greeted this second group with feelings of fear and suspicion that led inevitably to attack. The leader of the group, Fray Rodriguez, was killed, and the rest of the party returned to Nueva Viscaya, as the new province was called. In spite of the unfriendliness of the pueblos, two of the Franciscan brothers stayed on at the pueblo of Puaray hoping to convert the Indians to the "true" religion.

As was the custom, those returning spread stories of rich mines and great cities. Some also voiced fear about the fate of the two remaining missionaries. One wealthy citizen, Antonio de Espejo, offered to finance and lead a rescue party to aid the two Franciscans.

In 1582, Espejo was given permission for this errand of mercy. He gathered a small party of soldiers and servants and set out down the Rio Conchos. They followed the same trail Rodriguez had taken in traveling through western *Tejas*. When they finally reached the pueblo of Puaray, they learned that the Indians had indeed killed the two missionaries. This did not stop Espejo; undoubtedly, he was really more interested in exploring than in rescue. Now he encouraged his followers with another motive—greed. Espejo led them first eastward through the buffalo country, then northward to the pueblos along the Rio del Norte, and westward to Acoma and Zuñi. With a few Zuñis as guides, he continued westward a hundred miles, hoping to come upon undiscovered mineral mines. The rumors came back to waiting ears. Espejo had "with his own hands" dug up ore that was without question endlessly rich in silver! Further, he had followed another trail and come upon other mines (located near present-day Santa Fe, New Mexico). Espejo and his "rescue" party returned to Santa Barbara, their point of departure, by following the Pecos River and crossing over the Rio Conchos.

Espejo's written report of his discoveries was filled with exaggeration. But people read the accounts and believed them. Quickly, plans went ahead for the mining of this new-found wealth.

Acting without official authority, the lieutenant governor of Nueva Viscaya, Gaspar Castano de Sosa, organized a colonizing party of 175 persons. He moved them up the Pecos River and quickly conquered the Pecos pueblo and several other large ones, including Taos and Tiguex (Tihua). Soon, however, a company of soldiers under orders from the viceroy arrived and arrested the entire group, returning it under guard to Nuevo Leon, the seat of Nueva Viscaya. As has been indicated, the Spanish Crown did not encourage independent action or this type of initiative among its people.

Other illegal attempts to colonize were made but most ended like the lieutenant's party. Some would-be colonists simply vanished into the unknown. Many years later, scraps of evidence gave hints of what had happened to these careless adventurers.

PART II—FIRST PERMANENT COLONY

A Pioneering Colonist

Juan de Oñate was the son of an ordinary man who had made a great fortune in the discovery of rich mines. To him fell the honor of organizing, financing, and leading the first successful colonizing expedition into the lands north of the Rio Grande. Oñate was a veteran Indian fighter, having grown up on the northern frontier of Nueva España. He had also gained a great deal of influence because his wife was a descendant of Cortez. She was of "mixed blood," a true *mestizo*.

In his letters to the viceroy, Oñate proposed to enlist and provide an expedition of at least 200 men. He promised to colonize through "peaceful means, friendliness and Christian zeal" the lands to the north. His list of supplies makes it apparent that his main purpose for the venture was truly to colonize. In addition to wheat for sowing, he planned to take 1,000 head of cattle, 3,000 sheep, 1,000 goats, plowshares, bars, picks, wedges, hoes, sledge hammers, adzes, axes, augers, chisels, saws, sickles, and other building and farming tools. He insisted that the men with him were to bring along their wives and families. Additionally, Oñate arranged for six missionaries to convert and make peace with the Indians.

In return for his efforts Oñate requested that he be made governor-general of the lands he colonized. He wanted thirty square leagues of land (approximately 134,000 acres) as well as authority over all the people who inhabited these lands. He also wanted the title of *marquis*. For each of the soldiers and settlers he requested the title of *hidalgo*. He proposed that each should have the right of acquiring control over pueblos and their people. Under the Spanish system, this would make all Indians subjects of the Spaniards, meaning that the Indians would truly become a conquered people.

Oñate was granted his requests in full, although it was understood that the Crown's rights and its *quinta* were to be enforced. Thus, while Oñate was free to carry out his plans, he was completely under the control of the Crown.

Carretas Move Northward

Delays caused by red tape, indecision and lack of experience prevented the migration from getting under way until January 1598. Finally, the wheels of the *carretas* (wagons) began to roll northward across the rough and uneven lands of Chihuahua. The crossing of the Rio Grande was a sign that they were really on their

way. The river formed a natural boundary between the colonized provinces of Nueva España and the vast unknown lands to the north. Oñate in a complicated ceremony took formal possession of all the " . . . lands, pueblos, cities, towns, castles, fortified and unfortified houses which are now established in the kingdoms and provinces of New Mexico," as well as the " . . . mountains, rivers, fisheries, waters, pastures, valleys, meadows, springs and ores of gold, silver, copper, mercury, tin, iron, precious stones, salt" and so forth, with "power of life and death over high and low, from the leaves of the trees in the forests to the stones and sands of the river."[1]

The arrogance of this claim is shocking, for it shows beyond any doubt that the Spaniards and the *mestizos* had no regard for the Indian peoples, their lands, and their possessions. Such an attitude was common to the Spanish conquerors.

The main party moved very slowly because of its burden of supplies, equipment, and livestock. Oñate and a small group went ahead of the others to prepare the way. Everywhere they received a friendly greeting from the Indians. At Santo Domingo pueblo the Indians hailed the advance group as their lords and gave the strangers an elaborate welcome. In turn, the Spaniards offered a religious mass. The chiefs accepted Oñate as their great lord and took the new religion as their own.

The ability to adapt was a built-in part of the Indians' way of life. In religion, the Pueblos found common elements with the Spaniards: for instance, both their calendars showed religious celebrations being held at times of natural seasonal changes. In a spirit of cooperation, the Pueblos held their corn, animal and other sacred ceremonies on the days important to the conquerors. Thus, the Indians performed the deer dance during Christmas, the eagle dance on Epiphany, the corn dance around Easter time, and so on. The Spanish missionaries watched the activities with satisfaction. Obviously, the Indians were accepting Christian ways. The Indians were equally satisfied. They were continuing the customs of their fathers and grandfathers.

A similar arrangement came about when the Spaniards imposed their system of government on the Pueblos. The Pueblo Indians went through those acts necessary to satisfy the conquerors. Yet, under cover they continued to conduct the time-honored customs of their tribal government. Both parties were satisfied; the outsider was not even aware of what was happening.

To this day, the Indians of the Southwest have maintained their ability to adapt. After hundreds of years of being dominated by stronger peoples, they still have not lost their identity as Pueblos.

By July 11, the Oñate group reached the pueblo of Ohke, located on the east bank of the Rio Grande where it meets with the Rio Chama. The pueblo was renamed San Juan Bautista. On August 18, 1598, the main party arrived and almost immediately began to build a church. Thus was founded San Juan Bautista, the first colony

---

[1] Lynn I. Perrigo, *Our Spanish Southwest* (Dallas: Banks Upshaw and Company, 1960).

in what is known as the United States Southwest. Among the colonists were people of various backgrounds. Mainly they were Spanish, Indians of various tribes of Mexico, *mestizos* (Mexican Indians mixed with Spanish), and Blacks. These first contacts between peoples showed opposite forces and understandings at work. The colonists came to establish their way of life in what they considered to be an uncivilized and wild environment. The Indians of the region looked upon these strangers as invaders and conquerors who would take over or destroy that which they knew as their own.

The Indians were not prepared for these first encounters. Most of the Indians of the Southwest did not know the myth of the bearded white men who would some day come from far, far away and conquer them. This myth had contributed to Cortez's success in his conquest of the Indians of central Mexico. But for the Southwest Indians, experience was to be the great teacher.

The Spanish, however, had accounts, reports, and rumors to prepare them for dealing with the Indians. They expected the natives of these new lands to be "barbarians," which was simply a way of saying that the conqueror's way of life was civilized, while the Indian's was not. The Spaniards believed their culture to be much superior to that of the barbarian Indians. Therefore, they felt the responsibility of imposing on them those systems of social organization that are basic to a civilized people. These systems involved government, that is to say, a set of laws and rules that control civil behavior. Under the Spanish system, this civil control also involved religion, for there was no separation of church from state.

Government also involved land rights, property rights, dress, housing, customs, and ceremonies. Indeed, there was little that was not controlled or determined by the government or the Church.

It must be understood that the Spanish did not picture themselves as destroying a way of life. They simply believed they were giving to the Indians things which the "savages" did not have. To the Spaniards, the Indians were barbaric. They had no religion; they did not live in organized communities; and they had no regulated marital arrangements. Furthermore, they were not properly clothed, nor did they live in dwellings suitable for human beings. In short, the Indians lacked the necessities of civilization. The Indians should, the Spanish felt, be grateful to those who had come to give their lives light and purpose.

To introduce their version of civilization to the Indians, the Spanish simply outlawed whatever social systems the Indians had and replaced them with their own. In return, the Indians were to receive protection from their enemies.

Once established, San Juan Bautista served as the center for further explorations, for religious conversion, and for launching other settlements. Franciscan brothers were dispatched to neighboring pueblos to spread the word of God. Groups of soldiers were sent to explore the plains, some of them making contact with the peoples at Acoma, Zuñi, Hopi. Other groups sought mines; some of the searches were successful.

Occasionally, there were incidents of resistance against the Spanish overlords, but for the most part the Pueblo Indians were submissive.

One major uprising, however, brought such terrible results that for 80 years thereafter no serious resistance to Spanish colonization occurred. The event was brought about by the actions of one of Oñate's lieutenants, who attempted to take provisions by force from the Pueblos at Acoma. The Indians strongly resisted. In the resulting battle the lieutenant and 12 of his men were killed. When the Spanish survivors returned to San Juan Bautista, Oñate sent out 70 soldiers to avenge the deaths of his men.

Acoma, the Sky City, was built on the mesa of a huge promontory. It was a natural fortress that seemed unconquerable. But the Indians were not prepared for Spanish weapons. When the soldiers began firing a cannon into one side of Acoma, the noise and destruction so distracted the Indians that they left another side unprotected. The soldiers climbed the heights on that side, and within a few hours had destroyed the pueblo, setting fire to all the buildings and killing all who resisted.

When the battle was over, 75 men and 500 women and children were captured; only a handful escaped. The captives were brought back to San Juan where a quick and unjust trial took place. The punishment for having resisted Spanish rule was extreme. Every man over 25 had one foot cut off and was sentenced to be a servant for 20 years. The younger men were punished less severely, but they, too, were forced to give service to the settlers. The women and children were distributed among the settlers as slaves.

This harsh action brought a general feeling of security to the settlers. Soon the colony began to prosper and relocated itself on the site of a pueblo across the river, taking the name of San Gabriel. Two years later, San Gabriel received an additional 73 settlers and seven religious brothers.

Oñate dedicated a great portion of his time to retracing the route that Coronado had covered 50 years before. In 1601 he visited the great plains and the numerous Wichita tribes. On his return he found that some of the settlers had left the colony to return to Nueva España, where they were quick to report their dissatisfaction with Oñate's administration. They pointed to his failure to find quick wealth in mines or to succeed in converting the Indians.

Quickly, Oñate sent his own messengers to defend his achievements and his way of governing, but the attempt failed. In August 1607, Oñate was forced to resign his position. However, during the six years that followed, this bold man continued to explore and succeeded in following the Colorado River to its mouth, the Gulf of California. Even this important discovery did not save Oñate. The Crown totally disregarded his achievements and took away all his investments.

The Spanish Crown did not have to give reasons for its actions. Its strength lay in the people's complete acceptance of its absolute power. To the Crown, Oñate had acted in a self-seeking and much too independent manner. As a result, he had to pay the price for his "sins."

The colony itself was saved from a similar fate by reports from the religious brothers that more than 7,000 Indians had been converted to Christianity. This report inspired the king to declare New Mexico a royal colony.

The Royal Town of Santa Fe

The king's order made the colony a royal business. Now the Crown would take over the expense of maintaining the government and the military force necessary for protecting the king's interests. So the colony became not so much an economic venture as a religious one. The king felt it more important to save souls than to dig for gold and silver.

The new territorial governor resettled the colony some distance to the south, bringing them closer to large pueblos and contact with the Indians. The colony was given the new name of *La Villa Real de la Santa Fe de San Francisco* (the Royal Town of the Holy Faith of Saint Francis), a title which common use shortened to Santa Fe. The move, which took place in 1611, makes Santa Fe the oldest capital in the United States. Santa Fe can also claim to be the second oldest continuing settlement founded by Europeans within the United States, the oldest being St. Augustine, Florida, founded in 1565.

Slowly and weakly, the new royal colony developed. Its lack of economic enterprises or business strength was directly due to the influence of the Crown. Enterprise was not so much discouraged as simply not supported. But meanwhile the work of the missionaries moved ahead valiantly. One report states that 50 missionaries converted 63,000 Indians in 90 different pueblos. While the number of missionaries involved may be entirely accurate, one wonders about the astonishing number of converted Indians.

The religious brothers worked hard in their fields, ranchos, and missions in order to maintain themselves and serve their Church. To support their missions, they received tribute from the Indians in the form of labor. Each Indian was expected to give a certain number of days of work to the mission as painter, craftsman, gardener, herder, mason, weaver, artist, and so forth.

Additionally, the missionaries received a royal allowance. The *carretas* from Chihuahua brought in provisions and religious objects for the missions and returned carrying textiles, hides, and salt. This caravan of *carretas* was the only regular communication between the northernmost outpost of Nueva España and the civilized world. The *Jornada de la Muerte* (Journey of Death), as it was called, followed the Rio del Norte across the lonely, barren lands, crossed the river at El Paso (The Pass), and then climbed up the trail to Santa Barbara or Chihuahua.

As the missions grew rich, a separation developed between them and the colonists. The colonists felt that the Church held too much wealth and authority. They believed they, too, should have free labor. They particularly disliked having to seek Church approval for activities and economic enterprises that had nothing to do with religion. What resulted was a conflict between the civil and religious officials with each group accusing the other of having too much to say about the colony. When news of this disagreement reached Nueva España, the viceroy decided to hold an investigation to clear up the matter of responsibility for the Indians.

The viceroy tried to even up the control over the Indians, but the matter still brought trouble in the colony. The use of Indian labor was the key to wealth. For instance, Indian labor made the gardens, vineyards, and fields of the mission flourish and bloom. Indians tended the flocks of sheep, the herds of cattle, and horses. Indians wove the woolen blankets; they tanned the hides, worked the mines, constructed the buildings, dug the ditches. In reality, many of the Indians were little more than slaves. Indian labor was bringing into the wilderness those economic elements so necessary for keeping up Spanish civilization.

Some of the colonists had encouraged bands of Apaches to raid the pueblos near the eastern foothills of the Sangre de Cristo mountains and sell their captives to the Spaniards as slaves. It was a profitable enterprise for the Spanish middlemen, but entirely illegal. The Crown had issued many laws to assure humane treatment of the Indians. The distance between the frontier and nearest law enforcers, however, made it easy for people to ignore the laws. Indeed, the Crown's representatives managed to look the other way when such violations were committed. They knew that the measure of their success as officers of the Crown was the size of the royal *quinta*.

Gradually, the Pueblos began to react against the many ways the Spaniards were taking advantage of them. They also lost their trust in the Spaniards because of the conflicts between the missionaries and the colonists. Their anger rose with the continuous raids and attacks made on them during the early 1670's by the roving bands of Apaches and Navajos. The Spaniards had promised to protect the Pueblos, but they failed to do so. To add to the Indians' suffering, in 1675, 47 of their medicine men at San Idelfonso pueblo were found guilty by the Spaniards of performing acts of witchcraft. Four of them were hanged.

The others received public beatings and were thrown into jail. These were the holy men of the Pueblos. Without them, the Pueblos had no spiritual leadership. No one stood as protection between themselves and the evil spirits. The god of the white men had failed them completely. He had brought them only hunger, drought and slavery. He had allowed their enemies to hold the whip hand. In every way, the Pueblos felt themselves without power, without any help.

The Pueblos began to unite. As a group, they were a strong force. Together they dared to raise their voices in anger against the white men. They demanded that their medicine men be allowed to go free. If the white men refused, the Indians would do one of two things. First, they might abandon their homes and move into Apache lands, leaving the Spaniards without a labor force. Or second, they might organize an all-out attack on the colonists. The Indians outnumbered them ten to one.

The Spaniards heard the angry threats of the Pueblos and gave in to their demands. They released the 43 prisoners.

Popé the Pueblo Leader

Among the men released was a San Juan medicine doctor named Popé, who had come from the pueblo of Tewa. Popé had never converted to Christianity. He had held onto the old ways in spite of many beatings and penalties. For many years, he had tried to get the Pueblos to unite and drive out the Spaniards. Through all the punishments he suffered, he continued to believe strongly in the rights of the Indian peoples. Upon getting out of jail, he set out to organize and plan for a general uprising.

Popé quickly became the voice for the resistance, one of the first to be heard in those times crying out against those who would force their will on others without regard or respect for the cultural differences that exist among peoples. The voices can still be heard today.

Popé's biggest problem was to get the Pueblos to attack. Their custom was to fight for self-protection; they would not strike the first blow. Besides, they did not believe in banding together under a single leader. Popé used psychology to wake up the Pueblos. He made his people remember the past. Their holy men had been victims of the Spanish. Their brave leaders had been dishonored. They themselves had fallen into the trap of civilization.

Those Indians who had become part of the mission, that is, who had become "civilized," had given up most of their own customs. But the Indians living in pueblos not easily reached by the Spaniards paid no tribute and maintained their own way of life. They did not rely on empty promises of protection from Apache and Navajo raids. These raiders attacked both "civilized" and "uncivilized" Pueblos, destroying homes, taking food stores, sometimes leaving families to starve. The raiders then turned around and traded the stolen goods with the Spaniards, who asked no questions. But at least the "uncivilized" Indians could try to fight the raiders and could call on their ancient gods for help. The "civilized" could do neither—not without being accused of witchcraft. Had not Popé himself almost been put to death because he had returned to the old gods? It seemed as if the "civilized" Indians had given up everything for nothing.

Popé did not get the support of all the pueblos overnight. It took him nearly five years. He had to organize each pueblo, finding strong leaders who would accept him as their head. Popé centered his actions at Taos. From there, he constantly sent out messengers to all the pueblos. More and more, the feeling of unity grew. The single purpose of the Pueblos was to destroy the 2,400 Spanish colonists.

Finally, Popé felt he had enough supporters to launch his attack. Using runners carrying coded messages on knotted cords, Popé signaled his network of lieutenants that the date for attack would be August 11, 1680.

The colonists had guessed that the Indians were restless, especially around Taos. They knew, too, that Popé was somehow involved. Yet the Spanish were afraid to arrest him, for they did not wish to anger the Indians. The colonists had been in a weak position when they gave in to Indian demands about the medicine men and they were in a weak position now. They had no way of resisting an all-out attack. Perhaps, they hoped, if they did not take notice, the tension would pass. There were fearsome rumors, however. Soon, some loyal Indians brought reports of the coming attack to the Spaniards. When two of Popé's runners were captured, the messages were decoded and Popé's plans for attack became known. The colonists were warned of the date and told to prepare.

But Popé seemed to have ears everywhere. He heard of the colonists' preparations. Quickly he acted, moving the date of attack a day earlier than scheduled, to August 10. On that day, the Indians united in a great wave of destruction that killed men, women and children. Toward the missionaries they were without mercy. The few settlers who escaped fled to Santa Fe or one of the larger towns.

Soldiers fortified these towns as best they could. At Santa Fe the settlers were able to hold out against attacks and hunger for almost two weeks. At last, however, they were forced to leave, escaping toward the south where they hoped to join other settlers. But, as they hurried along the roads their hopes sank, for they saw only destruction and death. Finally, on September 13, they did meet other settlers who had managed to escape the attack. It must have been a heart-breaking meeting, with many exchanges of sad news and painful memories.

A few days later, this mournful company encountered a supply train traveling along the Rio Grande just north of El Paso. The whole group moved to a mission which stood across the river and made camp there. Later, this camp became a town, which is now known as Ciudad Juarez. In time, some of the settlers recrossed the river, starting a new mission. They built another community that was to eventually become El Paso.

An accounting of the uprising revealed that 400 settlers had been killed as well as 22 of the 33 missionaries in the territory. All the settlers had lost their homes and possessions, and all the missions had been destroyed.

This uprising deeply shook the Spaniards. They had encountered nothing like it before. The rebellion covered the entire province of New Mexico, an area of thousands of square miles. For nearly 150 years settlers had developed a region with a capital city, dozens of *haciendas,* and a long chain of missions. Now, in the first major setback of the growing Spanish conquest of the New World, the Spaniards had been driven out by the "barbarians"!

As for the Indians, they had thrown out the conquerors' God and had rejected the Spaniards' version of civilization. So fierce was their desire to be free of their oppressors that they had even acted against their own customs. They had united under one leader, Popé, and had been the ones to start the attack.

The man behind the successful uprising deserves study. Without a doubt, Popé was a magnetic man and a strong leader. He could inspire others and make things happen. He had made an impossible dream come true. He had driven the Spaniards out of the land.

Popé's actions following the victory of the Pueblos indicate that he would not be satisfied until he had also rid the land of every aspect of the Spanish presence. He started with religion. He led the Pueblos to set fire to all the churches and the great wooden crosses that marked the converted pueblos. He then worked to rid the converted Indians of the effects of baptism. With water and yucca suds, the Indians scrubbed themselves clean of Christianity. His next task was the destruction of the plants and crops introduced by the Spaniards. His people uprooted and trampled watermelons, onions, wheat, grapes, chili peppers, peaches, apples, plums, lemons and oranges—even those crops that were at the point of harvest. Popé also ordered the killing of animals introduced by the colonists, such as pigs and sheep. The horses, however, were set free. From these horses came the wild herds that soon galloped over great sections of the plains.

The Pueblos made an immediate return to the old ways and the old gods. It was as if the last one hundred years had never taken place—as if the Spaniards had never come. Surprisingly, however, Popé held on to some of the Spaniards' ways. He made himself "governor" over all the pueblos. He acted like a Spanish governor, issuing orders to the people and demanding that they pay tribute to him.

What Popé seemed to forget were his own words and beliefs. The various pueblos were not used to being unified and did not like it. Soon the people spoke openly of their dissatisfaction. Fights broke out between the different pueblos. To make matters worse, a drought hit the land. The handful of crops yielded a very poor harvest. As ever, the Apache raids continued. Popé's attempt to unify and rule failed. Quietly, Popé left. The pueblos went back to their old ways. Each watched out for itself alone. Each held fast to its own identity. More strongly than ever, each pueblo kept a tight grip on its ways. Never again would the Indians of New Mexico submit completely to the Spaniards, not even after the reconquest.

Most of the settlers still hoped to return to the lands they once had owned, but 12 years would pass before the Spaniards could re-enter those lands. During this time some settlers stayed on at El Paso, while others looked eastward, hoping to find a new life in the *Tejas* territory.

Tejas (Texas) had remained neglected since the time of Coronado. Some missionaries had attempted to do their work in these lands, but hardly anything was left to show that they had been there. One group of Indians, the Jumanos, did ask for missionaries to come among them. They were hoping not so much to be converted as to be protected against raiding Apaches.

More Indian Confrontation

In 1688, the territorial governor undertook the first attempt to reconquer the Pueblo Indians. A major battle took place at Zia. The town was destroyed and hundreds of the Pueblos were killed. Many of the Indians chose to die in their burning homes rather than to give up to the Spaniards. The governor returned to El Paso to organize the complete reconquest of the Pueblos; but his plans were cut short when he was replaced as territorial governor by Don Diego de Vargas.

Vargas was a nobleman who proved to be a most able conqueror and governor. In the short period of four months, Vargas and his army of 200 men took over 23 pueblos of ten Indian nations.

The speed and the extent of Vargas' success were made possible by the lack of leadership and unity once provided by Popé, and also by the courage and discipline displayed by Vargas and his troops. The lines of soldiers marched with such good order, confidence, and bravery, that they often took over the pueblos without resistance.

The Santa Fe colonists, however, had trouble coming back to take over the lands they had once owned. Whereas they had feared the soldiers, some Indian leaders still dared to fight the settlers. When the Indian leaders were caught, they were killed in the public square, setting an example for other rebels who would not accept the law of the Spanish Crown. Instead of backing down, however, the Indians fought even harder. Vargas pursued them into mountain lands, where the Indians were able to hold off the angry army for a long time.

The years between 1696 and 1700 were filled with the struggle for control of these lands. During this time, Vargas was accused by his enemies of having abused his office as governor. He suffered court trials, first being found guilty, then innocent. In the meantime, he was replaced by another governor.

By 1700 the little colony seemed to have a firm foothold in the far northern territory. More than 300 families had resettled there. The Spanish population now reached the grand total of 1500, the highest number since 1680. They met with little trouble from the pueblos. Even the last holdouts, the Acoma, the Zuñi, and the Laguna, gave in to the government at Santa Fe. Only one group continued to resist. These were the Hopi—"the Peaceful Ones."

The Hopi showed no signs of accepting either the government or the missionaries. One missionary, Father Juan Garaycoechea, did visit an isolated Hopi pueblo where he converted 73 Indians to Christianity. This conversion set into motion one of the most dreadful acts in Hopi history. Upon hearing of the conversion of the seventy-three, Hopis from other communities rose up in anger. Such behavior against their nation must be punished. They waited until Father Juan departed the community. That night the men from the other Hopi pueblos gathered together. At the first signs of morning light, they burst into the pueblo of the converted ones, setting fire to the homes and the *kiva*. All the people trapped inside burned to death, both Christian converts and faithful Hopis.

Only a few women and young girls were spared. By the time the sun was high in the sky, the pueblo was a smoking pile of ashes. The terrible fate of this pueblo kept Christianity from entering Hopi pueblos for more than a century thereafter.

The Hopi did offer to sign a peace treaty with the Spaniards. They asked only to be allowed to keep their religion, but the

Spaniards would not agree. So the Hopi remained an independent nation until 1850, when the United States took over the Southwest.

For 100 years more, nomadic tribes continued to raid and trouble the pueblos along the frontier. These tribes, including the Navajos, the Utes, and the Comanches, were beginning to move down from the north into the eastern plains. In turn, the Apaches increased their raids because they were feeling the push of the Comanches. These pressures caused Indians to walk great distances in their search for new lands.

Spanish law forbade Indians to use horses. Many missionaries had ignored the law and had taught trusted Indians how to ride. Soon Indians were far better horsemen than their teachers, some of them becoming cowhands and horse breeders. The uprising of 1680 had loosed hundreds of animals which the Indians caught and kept. Horses had great value among the Indians. It is easy to guess why. With them, nomadic Indians could travel quickly over great distances.

The desire for horses led to endless raids. The raiders, no matter how many sheep or horses they stole, always left behind enough animals to breed. In that way they knew they would have a new supply when they came to make their raids next year.

By the 1750's, the Apaches became a powerful enemy to the white man as well as to the Indian who lived as peaceful neighbors. Not only did the Apaches have horses; they also had acquired firearms by trading with French fur traders who were coming to the plains from the east.

The Spanish moved to check the raiding Indians and to act against the French who were moving into Spanish territory. Many military companies were sent out scouting into the plains and to the northeast as far as the Platte River. Commanders of these expeditions, such as Archuleta, Ulibarri, Valverde, Velez, gained fame and respect as explorers and leaders of men. They are also famous as the founders of great families whose members have continued to contribute to the history of the Southwest.

Because of these scouting parties the far borders of the territory were made safe. The colony of Santa Fe grew strong. Soon, other settlements became well-known. One was Alburquerque (now called Albuquerque), named for Duke Alburquerque, who was viceroy of Nueva Espãna. Two others were El Paso and Santa Cruz de la Cañada.

As these towns grew in importance, they became the locations for parish churches. Their establishment took away control from the religious brothers and missionaries and placed it in the hands of the priests and bishops. Up to this time the many missionary religious orders, mainly the Franciscans, had been the only spiritual leaders in the new territory. Now, bishoprics, or seats of the bishops, were established at Santa Fe, Albuquerque, El Paso and Santa Cruz de la Cañada. These frontier colonies thus grew to be great religious centers as well as lasting communities.

By 1750 the new colony, *Nuevo Mexico* (New Mexico), had an established population consisting of full-blooded Spanish officials born in Spain (*peninsulares*); Spaniards who had been born in Nueva España (*criollos* or creoles); a third group with mixed Spanish and Indian blood (*mestizos*); and still a fourth group made up of Apache slaves and Pueblos. The largest group was the *mestizos,* who followed a way of life that went along with the Spanish customs yet was different. Its difference took into account the geography of the territory, the way the territory had developed, and the make-up of the people who lived around them. These are the ancestors of many of the Mexican Americans living in the Southwest today.

Spain and its representatives now turned their interest toward the other arid areas of their northern frontier: *Pimería Alta* (Arizona), *Tejas,* and California. The Spanish now carried with them the knowledge they had gained from 200 years of colonial development in New Mexico.

3

Northward Movement

PART I—FATHER EUSEBIO FRANCISCO KINO

Pimería Alta

Pimería Alta (Upper Pima Land) became Nueva España's second-most northern frontier mainly because of the efforts of the Jesuit missionary, Father Eusebio Francisco Kino. Pimería Alta consisted of what is today northern Sonora, in Mexico, and southern Arizona. In topography, its lands are very similar to those of New Mexico.

Pimería Alta was named after the Pima Indians, natives of the lands between the Gila and Salt Rivers. The Pimas are also known as the "River People" and are believed to be descendants of the Hohokam (in Pima language, "those who have gone"). These Hohokam, who lived in the area about 1400 A.D., were very advanced. They built irrigation ditches, ball courts, and pyramids. They cultivated wide fields of corn and cotton. Where the Hohokam came from is a mystery. They may have been invaders from the south. For more than 1000 years, they developed their way of life in the river area; then for some reason the Hohokam migrated south again. The small group that stayed behind grew into the

Pimas and the Papagos. The Pimas continued many of the traditions of the Hohokam. They lived in one-room homes, produced pottery and built irrigation ditches to water their fields of beans, squash, and pumpkins.

Papagos in Pima language means "the bean people." They lived in an area which had no river or year-round streams. Therefore, they could do little farming. Instead, they were semi-nomads, living mostly off the land. Their name probably came from their habit of using wild beans as their main food.

To these Indian tribes, Father Eusebio Francisco Kino introduced Christianity. But Father Kino was not only a missionary and a church builder; he was also a ranchman and an explorer. He was the first white man to cross and make maps of the whole of Pimería Alta. In 24 years he made more than 50 journeys inland from his mission at Dolores in Sonora. These varied in length from 100 to nearly 1000 miles. He passed where no men had ever been before, or where signs of previous travelers had long since disappeared. His travels brought him through lands where unknown Indian nations lived and sometimes across waterless wastelands, which in later years became the burial grounds of nameless travelers who perished from thirst. One of these trails, which went from Sonoita to the Gila River, was called *El Camino del Diablo*, the Devil's Highway.

The records kept by Father Kino of his explorations and journeys were of great service to many explorers and historians. His map of Pimería Alta was the only useful one for over a century.

The hardships and barriers that Father Kino had to confront in his travels and missionary efforts make one wonder why he kept at it. If a man risks his life in pursuit of riches and fame, other men in other times can easily understand it. But to expose oneself to mystery and danger and pain for the sake of saving souls? This is not so easy to believe. Yet the salvation of souls seems to have been the only force that drove Father Kino. This same force put into motion thousands of missionaries, to all corners of the world, bringing not only a new religion, but also a new way of life.

Father Kino's first religious work took place in Baja California. In 1683, he joined a group of would-be colonists who sailed to La Paz. When the members of the group became more interested in the gains from pearl-fishing than in working for a productive colony, the Indians drove them away. Their second attempt at establishing a colony farther up the coast at San Bruno proved more successful. There Father Kino worked very closely with the natives. The records he kept make a clear picture of his feelings and attitudes about his work:

"Although . . . I have had very poor health and even yet find myself with little strength, I prepared the . . . pack animals and food and some little gifts for the natives . . .

In Tubutama this afternoon the branding place for 36 cattle was made. There are 50 head of sheep and goats and a band of mares, wheat, corn and beans for the Father, and a flat roofed adobe house with three rooms . . . This afternoon . . . at the peal of the bell, the people and the boys of the doctrine hastened to say their prayers with their native teacher in the same way as in any other old Christian pueblo, a thing which caused admiration and joy to the lieutenant. He said that it was a great pity that . . . these in Tubutama and those of *La Concepción del Caborca* did not have their missionary Fathers. There was a missionary Father at *La Concepción* a few months before, but he was removed with the . . . report that the Fathers at Pimería were here at a great risk to our lives."

Father Kino was a true missionary. To him, the natives were his wards, child-like people who depended upon him for their needs. He was eager to teach them and to help them learn those aspects of life that would "civilize" them. He was overjoyed when he found that the Indians would accept Christianity.

A few of the Indian groups adopted the new religion without protest. For some, conversion presented no problem; their beliefs went right along with Christian teachings. Certain other groups adopted parts of the new religion and mixed them with the older one. Conversion was not always based on a change in religious beliefs alone; the church offered protection. Each missionary group was usually accompanied by a band of soldiers. Their job was to assist the missionary groups in their two functions: to convert the Indians and to expand the influence of Spain.

While working in this area, Father Kino helped to found the mission at San Bruno as well as another at San Isidro. With a party exploring westward in 1685 he crossed the Baja peninsula at about 26° latitude and viewed the great South Sea (Pacific Ocean).

Discontent among the settlers eventually caused the break-up of the San Bruno colony and the people divided into two groups. Father Kino joined the one that sailed north to look for a better location. During the trip, they touched the coast of Sonora, but received orders from the viceroy to sail on and join the fleet that was escorting the Manila Galleon returning from the Orient. Word had come that pirates were nearby. When the fleet returned safely to

Acapulco, Father Kino learned that the colonization of California was to be abandoned because of lack of funds.

Thus it was that Father Kino was sent to Pimería Alta. When he arrived in March of 1687 he went directly to Curcurpe, a tiny mission station. It was a lonely outpost. Far to the east some important communities had built up around the silver mines, but Curcurpe then was an even smaller pueblo than it is today.

Fifteen miles to the north, Father Kino founded the mission of *Nuestra Señora de los Dolores* (Our Lady of Sorrows) at the Indian village of Cósari. It was located in a rich, fertile valley filled with streams. Today only the fragments of adobe walls mark the spot where stood the mission that was mother for a chain of missions throughout Pimería Alta.

In April of 1700, Father Kino founded *San Xavier del Bac,* which at present is a United States National Monument near Tucson, Arizona. Two years later he established the missions at Tumacacori and Guebavi, also in Arizona. As soon as a mission was established, he turned it over to others to care for and develop. This freed him to establish more missions. The three he cared for himself were at Dolores, Remedios and Cocospora, which stood at the extreme limits of the territory. When Father Kino was not journeying, he gave his time and energy to teaching, building churches and developing ranches for the support of his work. Here is a description of the Mission Dolores which Father Kino wrote two years after it was constructed:

> "This mission has its church adequately furnished with ornaments, chalices . . . bells, choir chapel, etc., likewise a great many large and small cattle, oxen, fields, a garden with various kinds of garden crops, Castilian fruit trees, grapes, peaches, quinces, figs, pomegranates, pears and apricots. It has a forge for blacksmiths, a carpenter shop, a pack train, water mill, many kinds of grain, and provisions from rich and abundant harvests of wheat and maize besides other things, including horse and mule herds, all of which serve and greatly are needed for the house, as well as for the expeditions and new conquests and conversions, and to purchase a few gifts and attractions, with which, together with the Word of God, it is customary to contrive to win the minds and souls of the natives . . . "

A man who could manage three missions, establish and see to the construction of others, continue to teach and explore had to have remarkable dedication and energy. Just his weekly visits to the three missions at Remedios, Dolores, and Cocospora amounted to a round trip of over 100 miles. In addition, Father Kino took charge of the trade between the missions and the towns and mining camps to the east.

Almost as important as Father Kino's search for souls to convert and "civilize" was his quest for a land route to California. For a long time he had supposed that California was an island. Then, one small event caused him to change his mind. The Yuma Indians made him a gift of some blue shells like those he had seen on the west coast of Baja California during his travels in 1685. If the shells had come to the Yumas from the "South Sea," there had to be an overland pass to the ocean by way of the Yuma country.

In 1700, Father Kino proved his theory. He traveled overland to the Colorado River and sailed down the river to the Gulf. There he had the Indians tow him across the water to the California side. Once on shore, he walked to a position opposite the point he had started from, navigating by the sun. Father Kino wrote in his records happily, *"California no es isla, sino penisla."* ("California is not an island, but a peninsula.") His overland exploration was proof of the very same discovery that Ulloa had made by sea in 1539, but Ulloa's find had been forgotten.

Father Kino was also a fine ranchman. From the small herds with which he entered Pimería Alta, he provided the beginnings of ranching in the area. The records show that Father Kino established ranches for a three-fold purpose. They supplied food for the missions that were starting to develop in California, they maintained the missions already working, and they provided an excellent source of trade.

On a modern map, one can point to at least twenty places, very important in the cattle industry, which owe their origins to Father Kino. It must not be forgotten that he was able to develop this new industry because he had the help of Indian cowhands, whom he had trained.

After 24 years of hard service, Father Kino had succeeded in founding 29 missions in Sonora and Arizona. After he died in 1711 many attempts were made to carry on his work, but few men had

his determination and energy. Also, the task had become more difficult for the Apaches who had been driven west by the Comanches,
now started to raid the ranches and missions.

In Pimería Alta, the process of blending two cultures into one
was well on its way. The Pima Indians, as well as some of the
other tribes, had adapted without much resistance to the mission
way of life. As they had done in Nuevo Mexico, the Indians of
Pimería Alta began to use sheep's wool for weaving. They now
employed the wheel and started to practice other skills and arts—
metal smithing, ranching, herding, irrigation, woodcarving (*santos*), painting (*retablos*), carpentry, brickmaking, milling, the preparation of new foods and methods for handling them. In exchange,
the Spaniards learned to cope with the geography in terms of clothing and shelter. They found different kinds of cotton and foods
such as squash, melons, and varieties of maize and beans. They were
taught to store and preserve foodstuffs. They discovered ways to
work leather. They soon knew how to travel without water and
how to find it. They learned how to look for ore and for the wild
plants that heal. Mostly, they learned how to survive in an un-
friendly environment. This was a land that seemed determined to
destroy the humans who trespassed on it.

After a generation or so the Spaniards accepted these learnings
as basic aspects of their culture. And as Indians and Spaniards
mixed, their offspring, the *mestizos,* were less and less able to
differentiate between what had been introduced by or adopted from
their Spanish fathers and Indian mothers.

For some years following Father Kino's death, few major
events occurred in the history of Pimería Alta. The missionaries
continued their work of conversion and of maintaining their existence through ranching and farming. The Indians more or less
submitted to and accepted the system that was imposed on them.
Meanwhile the Spanish and *mestizos* sought mines which would
transform them into *hidalgos (hijo de algo* meaning, roughly, man
of prestige) overnight. The discovery of a rich silver mine at
Arizonac in 1736 seemed to fulfill their expectations. But the mine
and others around it were soon exhausted. The event did provide
Arizona with its name. (The word *arizona* from the Pima language
means *ari,* few, and *zona,* springs. Indeed, Arizona is a land of few
springs.)

The mines at Arizonac brought in a new type of frontier
people who soon spread out into the northern territory—the prospectors. These prospectors, banding together for protection from
the Apaches, built a fort. Eventually the fort received military
support, making safe the settlement of a colony at Tubac, near the

mission of Guebavi. To the Tubac colony came the first white woman to make her home in present-day Arizona.

In 1751, the Pimas joined the Papagos to drive out the settlers. The Indians overran and robbed the missions of northern Pimería Alta, including the beautiful San Xavier del Bac. When the soldiers at Tubac restored order to the territory, the hard-working Jesuit missionaries returned to build up again the lands and buildings they had developed.

The Jesuits were a tough and demanding religious order. They were organized as an army, tackling almost every job as if it were a battle to be won. They were also devoted to education. The Jesuits started many schools and colleges in the New World. In these two important ways, the Jesuits followed their founder, Saint Ignatius Loyola, who had been a soldier and a scholar before he started the Jesuit order.

Yet in 1786 the Jesuits were commanded by the Spanish king to abandon their missionary work in the Spanish Empire. This change came about because of a power struggle between the Crown and the Jesuit order. The Jesuits were replaced by the Franciscan fathers.

The Franciscan order was completely different from the toughminded Jesuits. The Franciscans followed the gentle ways of their founder, Saint Francis of Assisi. Their main interest was converting people to the Christian religion, with less emphasis on education.

After the departure of the Jesuits, the Franciscans needed a number of years to rearrange matters, during which time the work in the missions and surrounding communities fell off badly. Not only did the missions suffer, but so did the schools and colleges. To make matters worse for Pimería Alta, the Apaches sensed the general weakening within the missions and settlements and in 1769, with an all-out attack, destroyed many missions, including the beautiful San Xavier del Bac. The garrison stationed at Tubac was helpless against the overpowering force of the Apaches.

PART II—ALTA CALIFORNIA

Men of Accomplishment

During this period of disorder and change, two outstanding personalities come forward in the history of Pimería Alta and Alta California. First was the Franciscan Father Pedro Garces. Using San Xavier del Bac Mission as his center of operations, he succeeded in earning the reputation of being "a second Kino." Father Garces was responsible for rebuilding this great mission, with the assistance of the Spanish architect, Ignacio Gaona, and the unending work of Indian craftsmen and artists. Their creation stands today as one of the great landmarks of the Southwest.

The second man was Capitán Juan Bautista de Anza, commander of the fort at Tubac. Capitán de Anza had been born and raised in Pimería Alta. He was a *criollo*. His father and grandfather had performed outstanding service for the Crown in the various frontiers of Nueva España, and the *capitán* knew well the problems and possibilities of this frontier. Like Father Kino, he strongly believed that an overland route could lead through Arizona to California. In 1772, Capitán de Anza proposed to lead an expedition to explore such a route. The viceroy of Nueva España agreed— for good reasons.

A series of missions and a *presidio* (fort) had been established in that territory. In addition, other events had brought new importance to Alta California. England had already driven the French out of the Mississippi Valley. Would she now push westward to drive Spain out of her northernmost border? As early as 1741 Russia had been sending expeditions to Alaska. Could Russia be on her way southward down the Pacific coast to challenge Spanish-held lands? The viceroy had the responsibility for keeping and defending Spain's possessions.

The viceroy understood that the chain of missions reaching from San Diego to San Francisco strengthened Spain's position in Alta California. The *presidio* had been established at Monterey. The founding of these settlements had been due mostly to the efforts and energy of Jose de Galvez, who had come to Nueva España as the king's *visitador general* (chief inspector). Galvez had seen the danger of English and Russian expansion into Spanish lands and immediately organized the details that led to the settlement of Alta California. At San Blas in Baja California, Galvez personally supervised the outfitting of two ships and the recruiting of colonists. He planned that the ships would sail north while two expeditions proceeded by land.

One overland group was headed by Fernando de Rivera y Moncada, who was accompanied by Father Juan Crespi. The larger group was commanded by Gaspar de Portolá, the leader of the entire expedition. Portolá was a soldier through and through, who looked upon the undertaking as a military problem. No obstacle was too mighty to keep him from getting the job done.

Along with Portolá went Father Junípero Serra, whose duty was to establish missions in the territory. These two men contrasted sharply. Portolá was tough and disciplined. Father Serra was gentle, kindly, and understanding. Yet both were completely dedicated to fulfilling their assignments. For Portolá, the task was to found two colonies, one in San Diego, the other in Monterey. These would act to block any foreign invasions. For Father Serra, the task was to make sure of the loyalty of the Indians, which depended on their becoming Christian and changing their way of life.

Portolá arranged for the three groups to meet in San Diego (one by sea, two by land). His map for locating San Diego was the chart developed by Viscaino in 1602. The first ship arrived in San Diego harbor on April 11, 1769, fifty-five days after its departure from San Blas. Eighteen days later, the second ship arrived. Of the entire group of crew and colonists, only two religious brothers were not ill from scurvy. Of the crew of one ship, all had died of illness or in the rough seas but two men.

In the middle of May the first overland group arrived. Their trip of more than 400 miles had been made in 51 days. Finally, on July 1, the main party led by Portolá and Father Junípero Serra arrived. The entire company was weary and weak from illness. But Portolá opposed giving in to weakness. He wasted no time in going

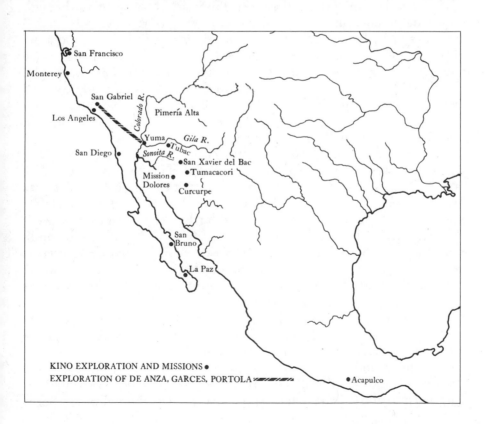

ahead with his orders. The settlements at San Diego and Monterey had to be established.

Portolá sent one ship with a crew of only eight back to San Blas for additional supplies. Then, on July 14, he and Crespi marched with sixty others northward to Monterey. Father Serra stayed behind with the sick. That march to Monterey took more than a month to complete, through what they later described as "ungracious" country. Although they reached Monterey Bay, they were not able to recognize it and so traveled farther, to San Francisco Bay. (Viscaino's mapping was quite poor.) They did not consider the site worthy of colonizing; in fact, the whole group seemed to believe that none of Alta California merited settling. Portolá realized that his men were so exhausted and starved that he must return to San Diego.

There the re-united company held out for nine months in spite of the constant threat of starvation and Indian raids. At last the ship from San Blas arrived loaded with provisions and supplies. Once again, most of the crew had been lost to disease or to the rough voyage along the treacherous coast.

Portolá simply refused defeat. He insisted on carrying through his orders. This time he sailed to Monterey Bay, leaving behind 8 soldiers and taking 16. Portolá's iron will was satisfied; even against rough odds, this attempt was successful. Portolá and his men were able to build a mission and a *presidio,* both of which were dedicated on June 3, 1770. Portolá had carried out his command; he had founded two settlements in Alta California, one at Monterey and the other at San Diego. He left Monterey, putting Pedro Fages in charge, and returned to Nueva España.

To Father Serra fell the immense task of establishing the Christian way of life in Alta California. The two little colonies made their start weakly and unluckily. Although the climate was mild and the area rich in fish, game, wild nuts and fruits, these foods were not familiar to the Spaniards. As a result, they were always faced with the threat of starvation. Even with these conditions the number of missions increased under the patient direction of Father Serra. By 1773, five missions had been built: San Diego, San Carlos, San Gabriel, San Luis Obispo, and San Antonio. Near each of the missions, a major community developed. Eventually, a chain of nine missions linked together the settlements of Alta California. Unlike those of Pimería Alta and Nuevo Mexico, these missions survived for nearly 100 years.

The founding of the famous nine missions was mainly the achievement of the dedicated Father Serra, who labored with all his strength against difficult hardships. Even as a child, Father Serra had never been really healthy. Then, just after arriving in Nueva España, he had been bitten in the leg by a snake, a wound that never healed and made him lame. Besides physical troubles, Father Serra had to overcome the hostility of some of the governors of Alta California. They did not like the independent way he worked. The biggest problem, however, was the Indians.

The California Indians

The California Indians were not like the Pueblos of Nuevo Mexico. They were greater in number, consisting of more than 100 separate tribes. Each had its specific territory with well known boundaries. Hardly ever did a tribe cross over the line of a neighbor's territory. The tribes were not warlike, but they stood ready to defend their own territories.

Most of the California Indians preferred to live along the coasts and rivers, where they could find plenty of food. Almost all the tribes made their meals of fish, shellfish, seals, sea lions, dolphins, and otters. They varied their diet with other animals, such as elk, deer, small game, birds, rodents, reptiles, and even certain kinds of insects. They ground up acorns into a flour-like substance and also gathered fruits, nuts, roots, berries, yucca, and sage. These first Californians were not an agricultural people. While the Pueblos had cultivated plants because food was not plentiful, the California Indians generally had a surplus.

The mild California climate did not demand much shelter or clothing. Most homes had a framework of poles covered with earth, *chaparral* (brush), tree bark, grass mats, or wood slabs. Their shape was usually like a dome or a cone. The men went naked or wore loin cloths, while the women usually wore short skirts and sometimes a cape made of grasses or skins. Most of the time they wore no foot coverings, except during cold spells, when they put on moccasins or leggings.

Unlike the Pueblos, the California Indians were loosely organized. They did have a headman and a leader of ceremonies, but neither of these men had very much real authority. Each family unit seemed to operate by itself. The family had a permanent home but often traveled to hunting or gathering areas.

Some writers call the California Indians a backward group because there are no traces of material products made by these tribes. True enough, they did leave little behind them. They did not make pottery, nor did they create complex weapons, tools, or styles of clothing. Perhaps such things were not important or necessary to them.

In the making of baskets, however, the California Indians were master craftsmen. Their baskets are counted among the finest in the world. The materials used included colored feathers and sea shells, and the designs were complicated and carefully arranged. The beauty and variety of these baskets are by any standards, whether old or modern, works of art.

The California Indians centered their lives around ceremonies and social customs. All the major events of life were celebrated with formal rites: birth, puberty, marriage, death, as well as seasonal changes. Celebrations took place in large, round houses and sometimes lasted as long as two weeks.

Another feature of the life of the California Indians was their love for storytelling. The people had a seemingly endless store of tales and myths, which they taught their children as a form of education. In this way, their beliefs and learnings were handed down from generation to generation in the manner called "the oral tradition."

The California Indians presented a strange problem to the Spaniards. Since they were content with their existence, what could the Spaniards give them that would be an "improvement"? The Indians refused all the benefits of a "better life," turning down offers of "trinkets" and "civilized food." They were attracted to only one thing—cloth. Furthermore, while they were generally peaceful, they responded to intruders with anger and force, although none ever showed the violence of the Pueblos.

For Father Serra, the work of conversion sometimes seemed to make no progress at all. The Indians were slow to respond to his teaching. Because few adult Indians would come close to the missions, most of his work was with the children. In time, the Indians came to look upon the missions as home. But such happenings were due to the steady and enduring work of Father Junípero Serra and other missionaries.

Newcomers Settle

The most difficult part of settling Alta California and keeping the colonies supplied was the sea voyage along the California coast.

The rough, dangerous trip took many weeks. Generally, the ships arrived battered, their crews reduced in number by drownings and illness. It is no wonder, then, that when de Anza proposed an overland route people reacted with relief and approval. Father Serra, who was in Mexico City at that time, heartily supported the project.

These were the conditions in Alta California when de Anza with Father Garces at his side moved out from the *presidio* at Tubac on January 8, 1774. This plan was to seek an overland route to Monterey and to establish friendly relations with the Indians along the Gila River. The expedition included 20 volunteers, 3 guides, some laborers, 65 head of cattle, and 35 pack mules. One soldier even brought along his violin, which proved very helpful in making friendly contacts with the Indians along the way.

The de Anza expedition headed west across Sonora to Altár, the most distant frontier *presidio*. From there they turned northwest, proceeding across the desert and through the lands of the nomadic Papago Indians to Yuma. This Yuman Indian settlement on the edge of the great sand dunes was headed by Chief Salvador Palma (his Spanish Christian name). De Anza realized the importance of winning the friendship of Chief Palma, for the Yumans controlled the shallow point where the Gila and Colorado Rivers meet.

With gifts and a long and flattering speech, de Anza won the chief's friendship and was permitted to make the crossing of the sand dunes by the simplest route. But even this was a painful and burdensome task, which at first failed. On the second try, a few of the soldiers and most of the mules were left behind in Chief Palma's care, while the rest of the party made their way around the great dunes, choosing instead to struggle through the rough mountain trails. On March 22 they reached the mission of San Gabriel, about 120 miles north of San Diego. De Anza's major accomplishment was in proving that there was an overland passage between Nueva España and Alta California. Father Kino had been right.

De Anza completed his plan by making a quick trip to Monterey. By May 3 the expedition was on its way back to Yuma. There they found that although the soldiers had deserted, Chief Palma and his tribe had taken good care of the mules and the supplies. They picked up their belongings and, following the Gila River, marched back to Tubac, reaching the *presidio* by May 26. The difference in traveling time was truly amazing.

By November, de Anza was in Mexico City being promoted to the rank of lieutenant-colonel of cavalry for his outstanding accomplishment. Father Garces was not there to share the praise. From Tubac, he had moved farther north to continue his work.

Now that the territory was no longer regarded as completely remote, a number of other groups explored and settled throughout Alta California. People soon realized that this new land offered many opportunities for growth and development. Because its great bay offered a perfect natural harbor, San Francisco seemed a promising place to start a colony.

De Anza himself, in 1775, led a second expedition to found a colony there. This group consisted of 240 people, 140 mules loaded with provisions, and an additional 450 horses and mules. Three Franciscans also went along, including the tireless Father Garces. Of the 30 soldiers who escorted the group, only one did not take along his wife. Those families who had children brought their young ones with them.

The journey was rough but they managed all the hardships, arriving safely at San Gabriel on January 3, 1776. During the trip the group had grown in number by four new persons. These babies were among the first of many culturally and racially mixed children to be born in Alta California.

The colonists continued north to Monterey. Resting there for two months, they moved on to San Francisco. They stayed at the Mission Dolores while the *presidio* was built to house them. On September 17, 1776, the dedication of the *presidio* took place. The settlement was started at the site known now as the Golden Gate.

De Anza and Father Garces began the return journey to Nueva España. At Yuma, however, Father Garces once again left his companion to venture across the deserts and into the San Joaquin Valley.

California, although a distant wilderness, was beginning to attract settlers. Among the more interesting settlements was *El Pueblo de Nuestra Señora Reina de Los Angeles del Rió de Porciúncula* (Los Angeles). A group of 23 people who had crossed the deserts of Sinaloa, Sonora, and California was granted permission to start a settlement on the fertile banks of the Rio Porciúncula. A more diverse group is hard to imagine. It included Mexican Indians, mulattos, Blacks, Spaniards, a *mestizo,* and their families. One man is believed to have been Chinese. By 1784, their mud huts, built in the Indian style, were replaced by adobe houses and the building of a mission church was started. This small community developed into a trade center along the overland route to New Mexico known as "The Old Spanish Trail."

Settlement of California did not go smoothly once the overland route had been established. There was conflict between settlers and Indians. As was often the case, the settlers treated the Indians rudely, with no regard for their rights or dignity. The Indians, of course, reacted to such treatment with anger. But although outbursts of hostility resulted in many deaths and much destruction, the colonies and missions held on. The peaceful times between conflicts allowed the exchange of cultures to grow.

Many of the missions added to their farming activities the development of trade among the Indians. The beauty of many of the California missions stands as lasting tribute to these Indian artisans. From the design of these early missions grew the kind of architecture which came to be recognized as "mission style." This style still influences building design and city planning in many California communities.

By 1800, California had about 1,200 non-Indian settlers. They included *mestizos, criollos,* mulattos (of Black and white parents), some *zambos* (of Black and Indian parents), and a very few *peninsulares.* In addition, there were about 20,000 Mission Indians, not a great number in comparison to the overall Indian population.

Mission Indians gave up their tribal way of life and moved into houses near the missions, or the *presidios.* They also owned *ranchos* or worked on those owned by the missions. The gentle California Indians did not hold to their tribal customs as strongly as the Pueblos had. Those who could not accept the new religion and way of life did not fight, but instead stayed in their old territories or established new ones.

The newcomers to California gradually developed rich industries. Leather and tallow were popular, as well as the production of olive oil. Part of California proved to be perfect for cattle. The mild climate, much like that of Spain, also allowed them to grow familiar crops, like grapes, citrus fruits, olives, and figs. At first, the settlers produced only enough to supply their needs, but success produced surpluses which could be traded at a profit. Soon the holds of Spanish ships sailing to the Orient also carried California goods and produce.

English trading ships began visits to the California colonies in about 1790. In 1806, a Russian vessel sailed into San Francisco harbor seeking food for its settlement at Sitka, Alaska. From this visit comes one of California's most romantic incidents.

The officer in charge of the Russian ship was Nikolai Rezanof. While trading for food and supplies, he met the daughter of the *presidio* commander, the lovely Concepción Arguello. Although neither could speak the other's language, he courted and won her in marriage. Unhappily, Nikolai had his duty to sail away, but promised his bride he would return to her quickly. Concepción waited, but Nikolai did not return. Giving up hope, the young bride became a nun and devoted her life to work among the poor. Thirty-five years later, she learned that Nikolai had died while crossing the frozen lands of Siberia. This account is one of many romantic true stories connected with early California.

PART III—Tejas

Slow Progress in Tejas

The Pueblo uprising in 1680 (Chapter II) had turned exploration and missionary activities toward southern *Tejas*. Again the interest in expanding into this new land was based on the search for gold, the conversion of the Indians, and the urge to seek new horizons. But these were not the only reasons. Another very important reason was political.

Spain needed to act against another power moving and expanding in the Mississippi valley—the French. The French had made early explorations in the far north around the Great Lakes. Following southward the course of the Mississippi River, they started a community on the delta at the mouth of this great river and called the territory Louisiana.

News travels fast. Reports reached Mexico City that the French had built a fort on lands claimed by Spain. Alonso de León was sent out with a company of soldiers in 1686 to drive out the French trespassers. De Leon searched for the fort for two years and was at last able to find it only with the help of Father Damien Massenet, a French deserter. The fort was located on the Bay of Espíritu Santo. When they reached it they found ruins, two bodies, and many dead pigs. There was no explanation.

Although there were steady rumors that more Frenchmen were present in the area, none was found. These rumors hurried the establishment of a mission and a *presidio* in 1690 at the Trinity River, not too far from present-day Nacogdoches. Here, as in

California, the Indians did not take easily to mission life, and the mission was abandoned. For the next 20 years, the Spanish attempted no other permanent ventures in the area. The French, however, founded Biloxi in 1699, and New Orleans in 1718 as junctions for their Mississippi River trade.

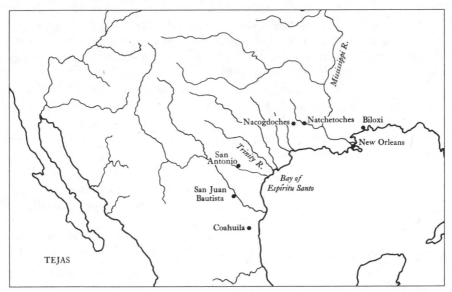

The circumstances that led to renewed and successful Spanish attempts to colonize the *Tejas* territory read like something out of a novel. A Franciscan, Father Francisco Hidalgo of the Mission San Jaun Bautista on the Rio Grande, wrote to the viceroy of Nueva España, requesting permission to extend missionary work among the tribes north of the river. When the answer did not come, Father Hidalgo, unable to bear the waiting, wrote a letter to the governor of New France begging for his help. The French governor knew that his country already had plans for starting trading posts in that area and was happy to grant the request. Such an undertaking would give France a strong foothold in these disputed lands as well as control over trade with the Indians. He instructed his agent, Louis Juchereau St. Denis, to meet Father Hidalgo and assist him in planning. When St. Denis arrived at San Juan Bautista, Father Hidalgo was not there, but Capitán Diego Ramón and his granddaughter made the Frenchman welcome. To make a long story short, St. Denis found Manuela, the granddaughter, much more interesting than the setting up of missions and trading posts, and even his loyalty to France. He courted and wed her.

St. Denis and his bride were sent to Mexico City, where the young Frenchman spoke frankly about the French governor's plans for extending French trading posts among the Indians. This information forced the viceroy into immediate action. He sent out Capitán Ramón's son, Capitán Domingo Ramón, with St. Denis as guide to establish Spanish missions in eastern *Tejas*.

The Ramón expedition to eastern *Tejas* consisted of sixty-five people, including nine Franciscan brothers, along with about 1,000 head of livestock. Leaving Coahuila in April, 1717, they traveled north and then east to the Neches River. In that region they built a *presidio* and nine missions. One mission at Nacogdoches was very close to the French trading post at Natchetoches.

At this point, St. Denis acted in a curious manner. He wrote a letter to the French authorities, telling them about Spanish plans for expansion. Somehow, the letter fell into Spanish hands and the Frenchman was arrested and returned to Mexico City. St. Denis escaped from prison, stole a horse, and rode back to San Juan Bautista, where he picked up Manuela. The two fled to New Orleans, where the French governor forgave his wrong-doings. St. Denis was put in command of a fort, where he remained until his death in 1744.

The Spanish missions near the Neches River, especially the one at Nacogdoches, had difficulty with both the Indians and the French. The great distance between these missions and the nearest military post, Coahuila, cut off their protection. Therefore, in 1718, the governor of Coahuila ordered the building of a *presidio* within reach of the missions. Capitán Domingo Ramón led his troops to a suitable point on the San Antonio River in south–central *Tejas*. There he founded the *presidio* of San Antonio de Bejar on May 5. At the same time, the mission of San Antonio de Valero was built. (Later in history, the chapel for this mission would be known as *El Alamo,* the Cottonwood.)

In spite of the building of missions, missionary work in *Tejas* continued to be difficult. The tribes were mainly nomadic and did not easily adjust to the life of the mission. The Indians made war among themselves, especially the Apaches and the Comanches. Religious workers always faced the destruction of the missions and the killing of their holy men. This in turn would bring on avenging Spanish troops.

All in all, the lack of progress was most discouraging. During 50 years, no more than about 2,000 mission Indians had been gathered. Each year the group grew smaller. By 1810, *Tejas* had only about 2,600 settlers and 500 mission Indians.

Political Maneuvering

All the time the French continued as a constant source of trouble for the Spaniards. They attempted to push through trade from the north to colonies in New Mexico and *Tejas* and were rivals of the Spanish in trading with the Indians of the Great Plains. One time, French traders even managed to push through a trail that led them to Santa Fe where they were stopped by Spanish soldiers. The uncomfortable fact was that traders from the northeast could now reach the new Spanish colonies. The French also provided a terrifying threat to the Spanish by trading guns and powder with the Indians. Once the Indian had guns and horses he was equal to any Spanish soldier.

The conflict between Spain and France in the New World came to an end in 1760, when these two powers allied themselves against Great Britain. In the war that followed, France lost, but before the war ended, she gave up to Spain all her claims to land west of the Mississippi. After the war, France gave up all its remaining land east of the Mississippi, and in Canada, to Great Britain.

Spanish control now extended over colonies that had French culture and language. As one might expect, these differences caused many problems. But there were benefits, too. For example, the Spanish learned how to deal with the nomadic Indians. The French custom of establishing trading posts produced far better results than had the Spanish missions. Therefore, the Spanish soon abandoned their missions in favor of trading posts, which eventually developed into communities. These communities served the Spanish as a second line of defense against the British. The first line of defense was the rivers.

All the great waterways of the far eastern lands joined the Mississippi along its course. The nation which controlled both sides of the Mississippi could control all trade and activities to the north, the east and even the far northwest.

When the English-speaking American colonies declared their independence from Great Britain, Spain saw its opportunity to rid itself of the British threat and moved to support France. By allying with France and lending support to the colonies, Spain strengthened its foothold along the Mississippi River, gaining control of much of the trade of the great river. Few actual battles were fought between the Spanish and the British.

When defeated England recognized the independence of the Thirteen Colonies, Spain received her reward. She gained all rights to Florida, but no additional lands east of the Mississippi River. But Spain now found another force to confront while it protected its American empire—the new-born United States.

The map shows clearly to what extent the settlement of northern Nueva España had grown by this time.

4

A New Culture

The 200 years that followed the founding of the first settlements in Nuevo Mexico brought a new way of life to the various northern frontiers of Nueva España. The combination of the Indian and the Spanish created not only a new people, the *mestizo*, but also a new culture.

A great deal of evidence exists today of the *mestizo* culture. Much of it has become a part of present-day living. Together with those areas of cultural merging already reviewed in the preceding chapters, this blending of cultures is probably most readily seen in the arts.

Arts and Crafts

The buildings dating from the founding of Santa Fe that still stand demonstrate an art form not truly Spanish, not truly Indian. They show the strong Romanesque-Moorish influence introduced by the Spanish and characterized by the tall, thick walls and round arches, the long corridors, the plainness of the exterior and the *patio* (courtyard) in the interior. Here and there are the modifications typical to the Indians—the use of local materials, the way the buildings fit in with their surroundings, the touches of style and decoration. Features of Indian architecture include adobe bricks and adobe frames, *vigas* (beams) for support, the repeating of the colors of the soil and the shapes of the nearby *mesas*.

What makes these buildings unique is that they look as if they are part of their environment; they do not seem to intrude on nature. A study of the details of a mission usually reveals the work of master craftsmen. These men were rarely Spanish; mostly, they were *mestizo*. They labored hard and with a sense of personal involvement that produced beautiful altars, doors, beams, pillars, frames, staircases and other structural details. Reference has been made before to the work of these skilled artisans, but repetition serves as a reminder that the communities on the rugged frontier were not lacking a sense of beauty and an appreciation for fine workmanship.

These communities produced fine painters, artists and architects. Many painters copied the masters of the Old World. More often, however, they expressed their own religious interpretations, particularly in the *retablos*, the paintings on tablets or boards placed behind altars.

Many of the *retablos* may seem crude and primitive, but their very strong and simple lines show how intensely the artists felt about their subjects. Some of the oldest of the *retablos* are the work of new converts. The mark of their culture is seen in the design and interpretation. This same evidence is seen in the *santos*, carved wooden religious images. The carvers of *santos*, who used native pine or cottonwood, became known as *santeros*. Some *santeros* became so important that they brought fame to their communities.

In the frescoes which decorate the walls of many missions, this intense religious feeling is repeated, not only as proof of the artist's faith but also as a way of making an object of lasting beauty. A visit to the buildings and structures dating back to this period develops in the observer new respect for a culture that is neither pure Indian nor pure Spanish, but both.

Mestizo craftsmen also used weaving as an outlet for artistic expression. The *mantas* (blankets) that this group produced were different from the Indian blankets, yet the designs showed strong

Indian influence. Most designs consisted of a maze of parallel diamond shapes, all having the same center and woven in six or eight colors. In New Mexico, where sheep ranching had developed to a high degree, the *manta* became one of the chief objects of trade. In fact, *mantas* were used almost like money.

Some craftsmen preferred to express themselves in leather crafting. Saddles were always treated with great respect, especially when they reflected the skill and talent of a true artist of leather. The working of leather and the carving of wood were combined in making furniture. During this period many lovely pieces of museum quality were created. The patterns carved into the great doors, panels and furniture of churches and homes remain a record of the meshing of the two cultures.

Poetry, Songs and Ballads

Literature did not offer a great outlet for such self-expression because the majority of the people did not read or write, a situation common in most parts of the world at that time. Among the *conquistadores* were many fine writers and poets, but they saw their new world through Spanish eyes. An example is Capitán Gaspar Perez de Villagra's epic poem dealing with the conquest of New Mexico. Here is a free translation of the first few lines of his work.

History of New Mexico
by
Capitán Gaspar de Villagra

First Canto

Which makes known the details of the history and the description of New Mexico; and information gathered from the buildings of the Indians; and of the area from which the Mexicans originated.

Of battles I sing and of the heroic man.
Of this man's being, his valor, prudence and great effort,
Of his endless, never-tiring patience,
Who over an immense ocean of annoyance,
Despite the fangs of foul, poisonous envy,
Brave deeds of strength he always achieves,
I sing of those brave men of Spain, *conquistadores,*
Who in the Western India (New World) nobly strive,
And search out all the hidden worlds.
Still onward they push their glorious deed
With their strong arms and acts of daring valor.

One can well imagine the pleased smile of the king of Spain reading this poem addressed to him. One can also see how the poet forcefully built up the deeds of the *conquistadores*.

The diaries and records of educated settlers and missionaries give evidence of a changing literary style which increasingly adopted words and expressions from the Indian culture.

The feeling for language and expression runs through folk plays. These were generally of a religious nature, and helped bridge the language gap between the missionary and the Indian. A few plays from Spain or Nueva España were rewritten to fit in with local traditions.

Not all artistic expression had religious themes. Some folk songs carried through with the Indian style of story telling, in which animals are personified or man takes on animal characteristics. In the following folk song, *El Coyotito* (The Little Coyote), the Indian style controls the meaning and also the word usage. Certain terms are Indian in origin, or New World, such as *coyote*, *jacalito* (small house), *nopalito* (cactus), *tuna* (fruit of the cactus).

El Coyotito

Cuando salí de Hermosillo,
    Lagrimas vine llorando,
Y con la flor del trompillo
    Me venía consolando.

Yo soy como el coyotito
    Que los revuelco y los dejo,
Y me voy al trotecito
    Mirando por debajo.

Ya se cayó el pino verde
    Onde habitan los pichones;
Ya cayó el que andaba ausente—
    Ahora veran pelones.

Ya se cayó el jacalito
    Onde colgaba mi espada.
Paque es tanto laberinto
    Si alcabo todo se acaba.

Ya se cayó el jacalito
    Onde colgaba mi espejo.
Debajo del roble encinito
    Tendio su cama un conejo.

Ya se secó el nopalito
    Onde íbamos a las tunas.
Ya me no más andaras celando
    Con tus celos en ayunas.

Les encargo mis amigos
    Que si ven a mí querida,
No le digan que estoy preso—
    Porque es el bien de mí vida.

A very free translation indicates that the song is about a man in prison. He imagines what changes may have taken place in his hometown during the time he has been away.

The Little Coyote

When I left Hermosillo,
    I wept.
I consoled myself
    With the trumpet flower.

I am like the coyote
    Who knocks them down and leaves them.
Then I go trotting off
    Looking downward (which deceives them).

The green pine tree has fallen
    Where the pigeons used to live.
He who was gone has come home—
    Now you guys take care.

The little house has fallen
    Where I used to hang my sword.
Why make such a big fuss,
    Since everything does run out.

The little house has fallen
    Where I used to hang my mirror.
And 'neath the strong oaks
    The rabbit has made his home.

The cactus bush has died
    Where we used to gather *tunas*.
You no longer can make me fearful
    Of your meaningless jealousies.

I entrust to you, my friends,
    That if you see my loved one,
Don't tell her I'm in prison—
    For she is the good thing in my life.

Songs and ballads were usually accompanied by a guitar or violin. But in New Mexico, shepherds developed a musical instrument, the *bijuela,* which looks like a giant jew's-harp made of a three-foot bow with a key and one string. The player holds the bow between his teeth with the string outward and makes a twanging sound by striking the string, producing a strong, sweet note.

Much of each community's daily life was determined by its particular industries or sources of income. The missions and the settlers had at first received considerable help from the Crown in the form of supplies and materials, but as each community became more stable and secure, it became independent and was responsible for its own support. Different areas built up various resources which gave them a dependable source of food, income, or materials and goods for trade.

Cattle Ranching

New Mexico's growing herds of sheep provided both food and wool. The former provided the thread necessary to make the *mantas* or a coarse cloth called *jerga.* A by-product of this early industry was the growth in developing dyes and looms. In New Mexico, Arizona and sections of Texas, sheep became the main source of income. To this day, some of the Indian nations depend entirely on sheep for food and income.

The most common breed of sheep was a small, hardy Spanish animal called the *churro,* which took to the new pasture lands as if it had always been there. Later, the *churro* was cross-bred with the Spanish *merino* to produce a hardy sheep which grew a rich, long staple wool.

The market for sheep was not limited to New Mexico. Each year a great drive made its way down the Rio Grande, crossing the river at El Paso and heading south to the cities of Nueva España. It is estimated that some of these drives included from 200,000 to 500,000 animals. In 1839, Francisco Chavez, New Mexico's leading sheep rancher, alone sent a flock of nearly 75,000.

Cattle provided income for the settlers of California. The livestock industry of the American Southwest had its beginning here, not in Texas, as most people think. Texas was originally an agricultural and sheep-herding area. As part of the Great Plains, it had been the grazing area for the great buffalo herds. Not until the buffalo were destroyed were cattle introduced into the area. From the few hundred head of Longhorns brought from Mexico, the California settlers bred herds of thousands. Longhorns, like

the *churro* sheep, were hardy creatures. Slender-legged and rangy, they grazed over vast areas far from the ranch. They, too, took well to the new land. Their meat was good, but their hides, horns and fat were of greater importance to the *rancheros* (ranchers).

Because of the Longhorns' long-ranging ways and the lack of fences, *rancheros* had to invent a system of identifying their own cattle. (Barbed wire was not invented and used until after 1870.) Their system, still employed throughout the modern world, consisted of *fierro* (branding), *señal* (earmark), and *venta* (sale brand). Each owner registered with his community's *alcalde* (mayor) the marks he expected to use. At least once a year, a general *rodeo* (roundup) of the cattle was held for the purpose of separating the cattle and branding and earmarking the calves. At the end of a day's work of *rodeo,* the families would get together for a grand *fiesta,* which included dancing, bear fighting, gambling, cockfighting, and, of course, lots of *barbacoa* (barbecue). This was the time to show off one's horsemanship or ability with *la reata* (the lariat). From these social activities arose the traditions that belong to present-day rodeos.

The Vaquero

Most of the traditions connected with the cattle industry had their beginnings at this time and in this area. For example, clothing worn by present-day cowboys is based on the outfit of the *vaquero.* His typical dress consisted of short trousers, buckskin boots fitted with large spurs, *chaleco de cuero* (leather jacket) and, sometimes, *chaparreras* (chaps) to protect his legs from the spiny *chaparral.* For warmth or protection against wind and rain, he wore a *poncho* (cape). Topping the outfit was a low-crown, broad-brimmed hat known as a *poblano.* The picturesque rodeo had other uses. It offered an opportunity for public announcements, for taking care of business affairs, and for informal meeting of young people.

Land Holdings

Possession of great tracts of land was essential to the settlers'
new grazing and agricultural industries. The Spaniards and the
Indians held widely different attitudes about the land. The Spaniards
considered the land a source of wealth. It provided the necessary
income for supporting life as well as buying comfort and luxury.
But to the Indians, the land was the source of life itself. Many
Indians thought of the earth as their mother; the sky, their father.
Nature was their religion. Their beliefs, their faith, their ceremonies
were closely tied to nature.

The Indian tribes reacted in various ways to the Spanish "right"
to the land. The Pueblos, who never believed they owned the land,
gave in to the demands. The California Indians were not tied to the
land either. Nature was kind to them. They did not have to struggle
to stay alive. The white man could have the lands he wanted. They
just moved deeper into other welcoming territory. But for the
Comanches and the Apaches, land was the provider of life. The
great wandering herds were vital sources of meat, clothing, shelter,
tools and weapons. If their access to the herds was threatened, they
would fight.

The Spaniards wanted to control the land. The metals within
the land meant wealth to them. They needed great spaces for their
herds and areas with plenty of water nearby to raise crops. In every
way, the Spanish settler saw the earth as his servant. Nature was his
victim.

The Spaniards did not recognize Indian feelings and values
relating to the land. They simply took it for granted that all the
land belonged to the Crown. The Crown in turn distributed portions or "grants" to its subjects for good service. The Crown could
take back a "grant" as easily as it gave one. As always, it expected
its *quinta*. (Special inspectors, or "watch dogs," made sure the
Crown was not cheated.)

Until 1720, land grants included guaranteed labor for the
landholders. This form of grant was called an *encomienda*. Under
the *encomienda* system the landholder received a huge section of
land, sometimes covering many square miles. These vast tracts,
especially when used for both farming and grazing, were called
haciendas; their owners were known as *hacendados*. The people
living on these lands became the owner's wards, paying him tribute
in the form of labor. When this system was dropped in 1720, the
settler was left holding only the land of his *encomienda,* for in most
cases, the Indians had moved away.

Land was granted or given by the Spanish Crown or its agents
in many different forms. Among them was the proprietary grant, a

deed to the land written in the name of the person responsible for
founding a new colony. For example, Oñate held a proprietary
grant. Another form was the community grant. In this case, title to
the land was held by ten or more families. Towns that existed under
such grants were called *villas*. In New Mexico and Texas, oddly
enough, Indians were given community grants for their villages or
towns, and these grants were known as *pueblos*.

Still another type of grant was the *sitio,* which consisted of a
square league (4,436 acres), used as grazing land. Grants of this
type sometimes covered hundreds of thousands of acres and were
often used by the government to pay off debts or to award favors
to an individual.

A study of land grant maps and the wording used in their
titles makes it clear that little attention was paid to accuracy. To
the officials of those days, the land seemed endless. Today, laws
require that land titles show strict measurements and descriptions.

The old land grant maps show topographic features such as hills
or rivers used as the boundary lines between the granted lands. In
those days, there were no fences, and people understood that cattle
wandered when they grazed. No one really worried much about the
accuracy of property lines or about keeping careful records. Later,
when the northern territories became the United States Southwest,
this relaxed outlook gave rise to many problems, some of which have
yet to be completely settled.

A man's land holdings and the way he made his living
determined his social class in the frontier territory. Social class generally divided into four levels. First and highest were the missionaries and priests who had behind them the authority of the all-
powerful Church as well as their rich, vast landholdings. Directly
below the missionaries and priests were the military officers and
their families. They represented the power of the governor-general
of the territory. The third and fourth groups were the land-holders
and the landless people who generally formed a master-servant

relationship. In California, the landed people called themselves *gente de razon, gente bien* or *los quien mandan* (people of reason, well-off people, those who command). The masters of large estates were known as *Dons,* and addressed as *Don* Felipe, *Don* Carlos, or whatever their given name might be. The *Dons* were generally men of mostly Spanish blood who were educated to read and write, held government offices, and controlled many laborers.

The landless people were generally the *mestizos,* families of soldiers who had married Indian women. Many became tenant farmers, *vaqueros* or ranch hands. Others became townspeople with various trades and skills to offer.

Personal servants or "slaves" were generally Apaches or other "savage" Indians who had been captured. The law protected those Indians who lived in the missions or pueblos against enslavement. However, when the *encomienda* system was dropped in 1720, the Indians who had been tied to the land were free to move away. Many Indians escaped Spanish control. Those who remained joined the *mestizos* to form a new source of labor for the *hacendados.* To ensure a constant labor force, the landowners developed the *peonage* system.

A man became a *peon* when he fell into debt. He worked for the *hacendado* and for payment received a portion of the crops. But a laborer needed more than just food; he needed such things as cloth, tools, meat, seeds for planting—items he could not grow. To purchase these things, he was forced to buy from stores owned by the landowners. Because the laboring men of the *haciendas* or *ranchos* seldom had cash, they had to go into debt to their employers and continue working to pay off their debts. Until a man paid off his bills, he was a *peon.* He belonged to the land. The landowner, to assure himself of a constant supply of cheap labor, required the children to pay off the debts of their *peon* parents. With the increasing *mestizo* population and the steady stream of newcomers, the *hacendados* had their labor problems fairly well solved.

Administrative Bureaucracy

The Indians and *mestizos* had little or no way of protesting against this unfair system. In fact, even the settlers were limited in the amount of assistance they could expect from government officials. The king's chief representative in the colonies was the viceroy, who was all-powerful. He appointed the governors of the territories, who in turn appointed his own assistants. Few governors were known as being humble or understanding; most showed themselves as proud, selfish and disagreeable.

These governors were more interested in making a profit for themselves than in stopping abuses against the people. Local officers, such as secretaries or notaries, were more understanding because they were closer to the people, but even they looked the other way when they stood to gain from a deal.

Three More Government Agencies

Below the position of governor, three other kinds of officers acted as agents of the government: the *presidio* captain, the *alcalde,* and the *cabildo.* In the *presidio,* the captain had complete power over the soldiers and the workmen who were attached to the post. In the town, the *alcalde* (mayor or justice of the peace) maintained public order, punished breakers of the peace, and "corrected" lazy or unemployed residents. In larger towns, the *cabildo* (town council) was the ruling body. Two of its members were chosen by the governor and the rest were elected by the town. The *cabildo* dealt out justice, directed public works, carried out royal orders and generally looked after the community. The *cabildo,* of course, had to get the approval of the governor before it could pass a law. There was a court of appeals called the *audencia,* but the one for the northern colonies was located in Guadalajara, about 600 miles south of El Paso and more than 1,000 miles from Los Angeles. It was difficult enough for a colonist of the northern frontier to get a fair hearing. For an Indian it was impossible.

Another serious problem for the Indian people was the language for few of them spoke Spanish. Although they learned to say prayers and sing religious songs in Spanish, they carried on their daily lives in their own languages, picking up only enough Spanish terms to get by with Spanish-speaking settlers. Indeed, most missionaries found that the best way to communicate with their converts was to learn their language. Deeply devoted missionaries translated the church writings into the Indian tongues, or worked out some forms of dictionaries.

The government provided special education for the sons of chiefs, forcing these young men to learn Spanish. On the whole, however, making the Indians learn Spanish was not a part of the program of "civilization." Spain itself was a multi-language nation. Each of her provinces spoke a different language, such as Catalan in the province of Catalonia, Gallegan in Galicia, Castilian (the official national language) in Castile. Therefore, Spaniards were generally bi-lingual, for they spoke the language of their province as well as Castilian Spanish. The American Southwest from its beginning has been a truly multi-language area.

The majority of *mestizos* retained more of the various Indian cultures than they did of the Spanish. The system of government, of laws and control, was Spanish; that which was personal and closest to the individual was Indian. This was simply because the system did not allow the *mestizo* or the Indian to be on an equal footing with the Spaniard.

Everyone understood that the colonies existed first and foremost for the support of the mother country, Spain. Therefore, it followed that all positions of real power and authority had to be controlled by those with "pure Spanish blood." The highest offices, such as viceroy, archbishop, captain general, were held by men who had been born in Spain. This practice, it was felt, would assure that the Crown's orders and best interests would be respected without fail. To the Spanish, a man with "mixed" blood, a *mestizo,* was inferior and furthermore could not be counted on to uphold the system faithfully. The Indians were wards, or savages, to be civilized. The Crown's attitude was like that of the authoritarian father who feels that he alone knows what is best for his children.

This system was strong enough to hold for over 400 years in some of the Spanish colonies. Among the *criollos* in Nueva España, arose feelings of discontent based on their inferior status in society. Living in the larger cities, these *criollos* were brought face to face with the differences made in their lives by ideas about "blood" and place of birth. Compared to the *peninsulares,* they had few rights and a lower status.

But even those colonists in the most far-flung outposts of Nueva España learned of important events in Great Britain's American colonies and in France. Great Britain had been roundly defeated by rebellious colonists and the French had overthrown their king and freed themselves from the ruling class. People were beginning to demand their rights.

How did these important events influence the frontier colonists? At first very little; they were too busy with problems of survival to worry about revolutions taking place in other parts of the world. But intruders from the East were beginning to appear. A new group was coming, outsiders who would have a great influence on the cultures of the Mexican frontier.

5

Strangers from the East

PART 1 — EARLY VISITORS

Growing Territorial Threats

Life in the Spanish colonies was very strict and closely controlled.
The Spanish were careful that no intruders upset the colonies with
new ideas. They especially feared the ideas that made possible the
breaking away of the American colonies from England. Thus,
Spain carefully kept all outsiders away. No foreign ship legally
traded with her colonies for nearly 200 years. After 1713, only the
British were allowed to land a single "permissions" ship once a
year. Of course, there was a great deal of illegal trade. By 1774, a
going trade had built up along the coast of *Tejas* which the government officials were careful not to notice.

For many reasons, California offered the best market for this
kind of trade. It was far away from central control. The coastal
waters were too rough and difficult for regular patrols. California
goods were desirable for exchange in the Orient.

Most ships that came to California were on a round-the-world
journey. The French began trading there in 1786 and the British
came in the 1790's. In 1796, the first United States ship sailed into

the California port of Monterey Bay. It was the *Otter*, captained by Ebenezer Dorr. The *Otter* was followed by other Yankee ships from Boston. They came to the Pacific shores to hunt seal and otter, and traded these furs in China.

Spain looked with mistrust on the westward spread of the Americans. To offset this threat she began to strengthen her northeastern frontiers and encouraged settlement there by offering large land grants to her people. Spain even went so far as to invite British loyalists (those who opposed the American Revolution) and French and German Catholics to settle the lands. In 1786, Spain finally opened its frontiers to Americans from Kentucky; and in 1791, the first land grant in *Tejas* was given to an American.

If Spain expected the same strict obedience from these "foreign" newcomers that it demanded from its own subjects, the Crown was to be sadly disappointed. The new settlers held little regard for Spanish authority, forcing Spain in 1802 to clamp the lid down on any further land grants to Anglo Americans. This new policy was to make little difference; the settlers came anyway. Many families made their homes in eastern *Tejas* as squatters, settling on unoccupied land without right or title. Some men came not to settle, but to investigate the possibilities of adding the territorial lands to the growing United States.

Spain's worst fears were realized after the purchase of Louisiana from France in 1803. The United States now claimed the lands lying west of the Mississippi River, into the area of *Tejas*, basing its claim on French exploration of the area. Spain showed a stronger case for ownership. Did they not have many settlers in the area? Had they not established control of the Plains Indians and set up trade relations with them? The argument between Spain and the United States grew more and more heated, almost erupting into war in 1806, in an area bordering the Sabine River. However, cooler heads took over and the troops of both sides drew back and declared the area to be "neutral" territory.

This incident was only the first of many like it. Fortunately, a real war did not occur. Neither country was really in a good position to fight. Each army was too far away from its central source of supplies and reinforcements.

From this period, Spain (and later, Mexico) felt growing pressure from the United States. Intruders continually crossed the rivers and moved into Spanish lands. Expeditions, such as the famous one by Lewis and Clark, caused the Anglo Americans to turn hungry eyes on the vast country held by Spain. Each adventurer came back with stories about the possibilities for great wealth in the far west.

Leaders in Washington, D. C., began to think of the United States as a country reaching from the Atlantic Ocean to the Pacific. Further expeditions were sent out by the government to explore the lands gained by the Louisiana Purchase as well as those beyond.

In 1806 President Thomas Jefferson put Thomas Freeman in charge of such an expedition. Freeman led a party of 37 men to find the source of the Red River, which was at that time the western boundary of the Louisiana Purchase. When Freeman's party was more than 600 miles west of the Mississippi River, the Spanish army stopped them. Freeman and his men left peacefully. He had orders from President Jefferson to start no trouble between Spain and the United States.

Other expeditions were undertaken by single individuals; still other by groups. Each adventurer hoped to fulfill the dream of an easy fortune. The vast area reaching to the Pacific promised a rich future to the individual as well as to the young United States.

The most noteworthy of the Anglo American expeditions into Spanish-controlled lands was that of Zebulon Montgomery Pike. Lieutenant Pike left St. Louis in June, 1806, under an order to escort some Osage and Pawnee Indians back to their tribal lands. Afterwards, Pike was supposed to explore the upper Arkansas and Red Rivers. Pike, with 22 men in his troop, fulfilled the first part of his orders, then went on to the Republican River in Kansas, which was in Spanish territory. News of this intrusion quickly reached the governor of Nuevo Mexico as well as the governor of *Tejas*. An army was sent out to stop Pike and his men. Pike learned that an army was coming after him. Instead of withdrawing, he pushed forward with half of his troop, sending the others back to St. Louis.

Lieutenant Pike and his eleven men wandered about the Rocky Mountains in the middle of winter. He tried to climb the mountain in Colorado that now bears his name (Pike's Peak) but failed. By Christmas, the adventurers were at Salida in Colorado. From this point, they worked their way to the upper portion of the Rio Grande. Here, they built a stockade. To find out more about Nueva España, Pike sent out one of his men, Dr. John Robinson, to Santa Fe. There Robinson pretended to be a trader pursuing a

buyer who had failed to pay his bill. No one was fooled. A troop of soldiers under the command of Bartólome Fernández marched out of Santa Fe and captured Pike and his men. Pike had the flag of the United States flying over his fort. The soldiers of Fernández forced Pike to haul down the American flag and run up the Spanish colors. Pike and his men were brought to Santa Fe under escort.

At first the governor of Nueva Mexico distrusted Pike. Possibly, the governor suspected, this was the beginning of a plan to invade his territory. Furthermore, Pike attempted to conceal his identity and denied knowing Dr. Robinson. But Pike was a warm and friendly person and soon formed a good relationship with the governor. He was no longer treated as a prisoner. The governor even gave the lieutenant a suit of clothes. Just the same, he thought it wise to send Pike to the provincial capital at Chihuahua.

The trip was a pleasant one for Pike. The Spaniards let him know that they would like to trade with the United States. Their only fear was that the American wanted more than trade. On the way, Pike was able to take a close look at the northern lands of Nueva España. After arriving in Chihuahua, he was sent to San Antonio and from there to the United States frontier community of Natchitoches.

Upon his return home, Pike spread his findings, publishing his report in 1810. To the people of the young United States, who felt that their nation's destiny was to expand from sea to sea, Pike's words brought great promise and excitement.

Events in Nueva España that same year brought such a destiny closer to fulfillment. The first attempt at Mexican independence took place in 1810 and was spurred by events in Europe which had caused a relaxation of Spain's control over her colonies. Napoleon had swept across much of Europe, conquering many countries, including Spain. Although the government of Nueva España remained loyal to the Crown for the most part, and efforts to honor the Crown's laws were continued, freedom increased.

For example, industries in Nueva España could now produce goods to compete with those of the mother country. In addition, censorship was lifted. Literature that expressed the new spirit of man's rights filtered through to the colonies. Colonial printing presses began to turn out reading matter that made people think and question.

Revolutionary Activities

The relaxation of controls provided the environment for the *criollo* priest, Miguel Hidalgo y Costilla, to lead the first effort for the freedom of Nueva España. Father Hidalgo was the parish priest of the small town of Dolores. A highly educated person, he believed strongly in the rights of man. He was respected and loved by the Indians of his parish. Contrary to the laws of Spain, he trained them in skills such as the cultivation of olive trees and how to make oil from the olives. He taught them to plant mulberry trees and raise silkworms. He also showed them how to manufacture pottery and leather products.

To punish Father Hidalgo, the authorities closed the pottery and leather factories and cut down the precious trees. But Father Hidalgo continued to teach the Indians of his parish. He also joined a study group for discussions about freedom and human rights. The group read and talked about the examples of the American and French revolutions. They also considered how to go about freeing Nueva España from Spanish oppression. All of them knew that such revolutionary activity was illegal and dangerous.

Father Hidalgo, despite his 60 years, became their leader. He inspired the others. Had the thirteen English colonies not won their freedom from a strong mother country? Now was the time to rise up against a weakened, captive Spain.

Many people in Nueva España wanted freedom. But would they join Father Hidalgo? The brave priest did not wait for answers. On September 16, 1810, from the parish church at Dolores, Father Hidalgo shouted the cry for independence. His cry came to be known as *el grito de Dolores*. But while the call was powerful, the people were not ready; Father Hidalgo did not have the following he expected. Besides, the Spanish government in Nueva España was as yet too strong, as was the army. Thus, the first attempt at Mexican independence from Spain was a failure. Father Hidalgo was shot by the Spanish army for his "act of treason." It was not until eleven years later that *el grito* of Father Hidalgo was fully answered.

Napoleon was defeated in the Battle of the Nations at Leipzig, and the Spanish king returned to his throne in 1814. The king expected that all would be as it had been before, but unfortunately for him, too much had taken place during the seven-year absence of his authority. The people in the colonies had tasted some self-government, had prospered with the new industries, and most important, had learned that they had natural human rights not granted to them by a king.

Revolutionary disturbances in and around Mexico City were useful to the intruders from the east. Many easterners supported the revolutionists, hoping that revolutionary activities would distract the Spanish government and thus allow the newcomers to gain a firm foothold in these lands. Ambitious men saw opportunities for establishing trade or other money-making enterprises there.

The California territory became a prime target for foreign attempts at takeover and liberation. Many adventurers took up the cause of independence from Spanish rule. One such man was Hippolyte de Bouchard, captain of a ship out of Baltimore. De Bouchard's ship, accompanied by a British vessel, left Hawaii in the fall of 1818. De Bouchard's plan was to land on the California coast and liberate the *Californios* from Spanish rule. However, the *Californios* did not understand de Bouchard's good intentions and resisted his forces. In the battle de Bouchard captured Monterey, stripped it of its riches and burned it. He continued down the coast, meeting resistance everywhere. Finally, he gave up and turned his attention to aiding those who were struggling for independence in South America. California had defended itself well against its first foreign invasion.

Another attempt at liberation in 1819—this time of *Tejas*—also failed. Led by "General" James Long and an army of Mississippians, the group planned to take over *Tejas* before the United States and Spain forged a treaty by which the United States was to give up any claims to that territory. Long's army increased with the support of Mexicans eager for *Tejas* independence from Spain. At Nacogdoches the Spanish army routed Long, who marched on to "liberate" Goliad. By the time Long's army reached Goliad, Mexico had gained her independence from Spain. *Tejas,* free from Spain's control, was now Mexican territory. Long refused to abandon his plan and chose to fight for the control of Goliad. The Mexicans, fighting under their new flag, won the battle and imprisoned Long and his men. Later, Long was shot by a sentry.

The treaty between the United States and Spain was completed in 1822. In American history it is known as the Florida Treaty, by which the United States acquired Florida, and Spain dropped all claims to Oregon. In return, the United States gave up all claims to land west of the Mississippi River.

While these negotiations went on, the colonists of Nueva España succeeded in their struggle for freedom. The newly independent country, *Los Estados Unidos de México* (The United States of Mexico), was proclaimed on September 16, 1821, eleven years to the day after Father Hidalgo's *el grito de Dolores.*

Their struggle for freedom had been as difficult and bloody as that of the English colonists. *El grito,* a loud echo for ten years, had inspired many leaders. Most of them were *mestizos* from humble backgrounds. Few had the education of Father Hidalgo. But they did have what he lacked: fighting know-how. They were not Indian fighters with *machetes,* knives, and bows and arrows. These were organized guerrilla fighters mounted on horses. Everywhere the guerrillas were active. This kind of warfare proved most effective. It was led by such heroes as Matamoros, a village priest; Guerrero, the son of a *peon;* the Galeano brothers, ranchers; the Bravos, *criollo* landowners.

One revolutionary almost as beloved as Father Hidalgo was José María Morelos, also a village priest. Father Morelos was a *mestizo* barely five feet tall, but powerfully built. A quiet, humble man, he had worked in the fields as a *peon* for almost 25 years. All his life he suffered from malaria and terrible headaches. Yet this man was greatly responsible for the successful outcome of the revolution. Some historians have called him a military genius. Others have praised him as the political guiding spirit of the birth of the new nation. Like Hidalgo and so many of the other outstanding leaders of the fight for freedom, Morelos paid with his life for what the Spanish called treason.

The new government of Mexico accepted the settlement and the boundary lines as outlined in the Florida Treaty. Mexico desired peace above all and the chance to establish a firm government within the country.

The wars for independence had taken place mainly in the central part of Mexico where the power of Spain was most strongly felt. The leaders of the revolution, realizing that the collapse of the focal point of Spanish control would mean the freedom of all Mexico, concentrated their efforts closest to the seat of government—Mexico City. Little contact or involvement had ever existed between the people of central Mexico and the colonists of the far northern territories. This lack of communication had led the colonists to identify more strongly with their region than with the whole country. Residents of California thought themselves to be not so much Mexicans as *Californios* and those of *Tejas* as *Tejanos.*

The Independence of Mexico in 1821 brought great changes to the northern part of that country. First, the boundary between this area and the United States became clearly marked. Second, the area opened up for new economic enterprises and settlement; re-

strictions and heavy controls were lifted. Third, this was the year
that the Santa Fe Trail was opened, allowing fur traders to come
into New Mexico. These changes were to affect Texas and New
Mexico in separate ways.

Cultural Contrasts

In Texas, Stephen F. Austin obtained permission from the Mexican
government to establish 222 Anglo American families in a fertile tract of land along the Brazos River. The grant required that
the settlers become Catholics and pledge allegiance to Mexico. Each
head of a family received 177 acres for farming and 4,420 acres
for grazing. In all, the Austin colony was given well over a million
acres of land. Austin was awarded the rank of lieutenant-colonel
and the power to deal out justice and provide for defense against
the Indians.

Mexico, anxious to populate its northern territories for
economic development, passed a colonization law in 1825. By this
law, grants were made for starting colonies in this vast, nearly
empty land. Those who received land grants of this type were
called *impresarios*. By 1832 Mexico had made about 20 of these
impresario grants, which covered almost the entire area of Texas
and provided for about 9,000 families. As early as 1830, about
20,000 people lived there, including slaves. Most settlers came
from the tired cotton lands of the South; a few from New England
and the Middle States.

Mexico's open-handed attitude towards colonization encouraged a flood of immigrants, who poured in by land and sea.
Many took *el Camino Real,* the old royal highway from Natchitoches to San Antonio. Others landed at ports along the Gulf coast.
The first settlers in the new lands suffered the usual problems—
language difficulties, lack of good roads, hostile Indians, failure to
understand or get along with a different system of government.
Furthermore, not all of the settlers had the same idea about
making a success of the new colony. Some were adventurers looking
only for fast money. Nevertheless, the Anglo American colonies
prospered. By the end of ten years, cotton and cattle were important
industries. Cotton depended on slave labor, while the cattle industry
relied on Mexican know-how.

The Mexican residents in Texas at first were understandably
troubled about the Anglo American immigrants, but gradually
friendly relations came about. A mutual exchange of learning
began to take place. By 1834, Anglo Americans outnumbered the
Mexican population by about four to one, spurring the Mexican
government to encourage Mexican immigration to the Texas lands.

While Texas developed and prospered, Nuevo Mexico was going through its own kind of changes. Trading attracted the Anglo Americans to Nuevo Mexico. Their great avenue of commerce was the Santa Fe Trail which connected Santa Fe with the Missouri River and on to the entire Mississippi River system.

William Becknell opened the Santa Fe Trail on November 13, 1821. On this day, Becknell led his train of pack mules into Santa Fe having left Franklin, Missouri, about six weeks before. By November 16, he had sold out at a good profit. When he returned to Franklin in February, he showed off his bags of silver dollars. News flew like the wind that trade with Mexico was open.

The next year Becknell took to the trail again in the company of twenty-two men and three wagons. These wagons were the first wheels to roll over the Great Plains to Santa Fe. The years that followed saw a rich trade grow between the Mexicans and the

Anglo Americans. The trade followed a definite pattern. In May the American traders gathered at Independence, Missouri. From there the wagon trains fell in line along the way so that at Council Grove, about 120 miles farther southwest, they formed one long train. There the men would elect their leaders and make their plans for protection, for the threat of Indian attack was always with them. The trail, approximately 800 miles long, took them almost two months to cover before reaching Santa Fe.

Santa Fe in the 1820's was not a far-famed or large city. It was to the Mexican not much more than a pueblo, a small town. In all, there were not more than about 150 buildings and homes of various sizes. The center of the *pueblo* had a *plaza* or square space. The plaza was surrounded on four sides by some good-sized one-story buildings. Each building had within it a large *patio,* a garden center. The colonists of Santa Fe built their homes in Spanish style but used Indian materials and methods of construction.

The governor's palace faced the north side of the plaza. Directly behind the palace stood the soldiers' barracks and the stables. The Rio de Santa Fe flowed a short distance from the plaza, but it was a dry bed most of the year. Several roads led out of the pueblo. Along these roads, the colonists had built their homes, almost all in the Spanish style. Within one block of the plaza was the cathedral with its own grounds. The areas between government buildings, the houses, the cathedral and its chapels were planted in corn or other vegetation.

Santa Fe served as the center for an agricultural, sheepherding and mining community. People lived in the outlying *ranchos* or *haciendas* and came to town only on special occasions. Most Santa Fe residents provided some form of trade or special service for the people living and working in the distant community.

The people of Santa Fe had a way of life in keeping with the climate and conditions of that area. Their manners and customs were Mexican. Their food mixed Indian and Spanish tastes and elements. In general an Anglo American entering Santa Fe would immediately realize that the way of life here was completely different from his own. The Anglo American was probably startled by many unfamiliar aspects. The first surprise could have been the location of the pueblo. The land was barren and arid. Far to the northeast were the Sangre de Cristo mountains, and holding Santa Fe as if in a cup was a *mesilla,* a table land. A second shock probably came as the Anglo American saw houses of blinding white adobe with the sharp green contrast of corn fields against them. There were very few trees to be seen. A third sense of strangeness must have come as he met the people. The people looked different. Their skin was dark and bronzed. They spoke a different language. They laughed and sang for no good reason.

The differences among the two cultures met in the custom of *fiesta.* To the Mexicans of this hard dry land, nature provided few pleasures. As a result, the Mexicans would often and without much effort hold a *fiesta.* To the Anglo American raised in the Puritan tradition, such an amount of party making was "high living." For

a woman to dance a *fandango* was not proper, even a scandal. (A *fandango* was a dance of Moorish origin that "made no effort to conceal what dancing was all about.")

Another puzzle to the man from the East was the way Mexican men treated Mexican women. Generally, the Mexican husbands kept their wives and daughters at home. The men felt free to roam the town, talking, enjoying each others' company and drinking. Women came to family type *fiestas* only. A woman in a saloon gave away her right to be looked on as moral or good.

The Anglo American found the Mexican men dashing and colorful. Their manners were polite and courteous. Nearly all Mexicans were excellent horsemen. Somehow, Mexican men, although they did business, never seemed to be at work. In other words, the Anglo American saw contradictions in the way of life in Santa Fe. He did not understand it. Where it was too different from his way, he looked down upon it. Yet, what he did understand, he came to admire.

In matters that involved hospitality, courtesy, comfortable living and education, the Anglo American accepted and even admired the people of Santa Fe. He limited this approval to the rich. In the poor people, he saw only filth, grease, lazy living and immorality. The Anglo American, usually a mountain man, adventurer or trader, had rarely contacted rich people in his life. This opportunity to be with wealthy people opened his eyes to the good life he wanted to possess. At the same time, the Mexican did not regard the Anglo American as an attractive human being. Most Anglo American traders came into Santa Fe right off the trail, with several weeks of dust and grime on them. They dressed in the skins of animals; they spoke a strange language; their manners were rough and rude. They boasted and bragged about making profits. Their major interest seemed to be getting money fast. To the Mexican, the Anglo Americans were a bad mixture of greed and vulgar manners.

Proper Mexican families refused to have contact with these strangers. The men did business with them only to gain some prized or necessary goods. An *hacendado* might come to town to buy some cotton or wool woven materials, guns or cast iron pots from the trader. He would not invite the trader into his home for dinner or to meet his family. Upon closing the deal the Mexican might share a drink with the trader. The Mexican made no offer of friendship. However, if the Mexican considered an Anglo to be his social equal he would extend all hospitality possible.

Reading the accounts written by the first Anglo Americans to meet the Mexicans makes clear the relationships among the people.

Anglo Americans who arrived as representatives of the United States government wrote favorably of their experiences. Other Anglo Americans of polite or educated backgrounds had similar experiences. Those of somewhat limited backgrounds recorded bad and even ugly encounters with the Mexicans. To this latter group, Santa Fe was a wicked town. They wrote down their misunderstandings. Some of these records and reports were published in the East. These first-hand accounts of the new land received wide circulation. People believed whatever they read. In such small ways began the misunderstandings and misinformation that existed about Mexicans and Indians and their ways of life. As nearly always happens when different cultures confront one another, neither draws an accurate picture of the other.

The trade between the Mexicans and Anglo Americans depended on cotton goods, woolens, and hardware which the traders brought. The Mexican women preferred the colorful cotton and woolen materials from the factories of New England to those produced in Mexico. The Mexicans sold animal skins, buffalo robes, horses, and mules. Mules became an important item. Although Missouri gained fame for the "Missouri" mule, the animal actually had its origin in Mexico.

Trading became a thriving business; a Yankee trader could easily sell his goods for six times what he had paid for them. Adventurous traders extended their business into areas beyond Santa Fe, some going as far south as Chihuahua. But the Santa Fe Trail always had the greatest traffic. To this day the traveler can see the wheel ruts made by the countless wagons that rolled their way into and out of Santa Fe.

PART II — MORE STRANGERS FROM THE EAST

Trappers and Traders

The opening up of the Mexican territory also brought the "mountain men." They were rough and harsh "loners" who made their living from trapping beavers and other animals. They came in great numbers, and most used Taos, New Mexico as their center of operations. They trapped beaver so completely in this area that in 1826 the Mexican government ordered them to stop.

Most mountain men followed the rivers deep into the south, while others went as far west as California. One of these latter, James Ohio Pattie, was arrested by the Mexican government in San Diego. When he returned to the United States he wrote a book about his adventures, *The Personal Narrative of James O. Pattie of Kentucky*. It became a best seller, filled with Pattie's interpretations of the West. The book reflected the bitterness and discouragement of his experiences in California. One can read as much between the lines in this quotation:

> ". . . this province would be among the richest of the Mexican country, if it were inhabited by an enlightened, enterprising and industrious people. Nothing can exceed the indolence of the actual inhabitants. The only point in which I ever saw them display any activity is throwing lasso, and in horsemanship. In this I judge, they surpass all other people. Their great business and common pursuit, is in noosing and taming wild horses and cattle."

It is obvious that Pattie knew nothing about the cattle business or ranching. Like most of the Anglo Americans, Pattie did approve of the ladies:

> "It may be imagined that we did not cut a particular dandy-like figure, among people, many of whom were rich and would be considered well dressed anywhere. Notwithstanding this, it is a strong proof of their politeness, that we were civilly treated by the ladies and had the pleasure of dancing with the handsomest and richest of them."

Pattie failed to explain how these rich Mexicans could become so if they were as lazy as he described them in the previous paragraph.

Two famous trappers who explored and forged routes to California were Jedediah Smith and Kit Carson. Smith's travels brought him through Utah and Nevada, while Carson came by way of Arizona. Both parties, Smith in 1826–1827 and Carson in 1829, reached San Gabriel, California; and both were forced to leave after difficulties with mission officials.

Other trappers opened up other trails and routes to the Pacific. Among them was Antonio Armijo, a Mexican who headed a trading company in Santa Fe. Armijo and his group re-opened a forgotten route between Utah and California that came to be known as the "Old Spanish Trail." Trailblazing was not new to the Mexicans. They had opened routes to mines and missions throughout the Southwest.

The Spanish Trail was a centuries-old path probably begun and used by Indians. Similar trails were the Santa Fe and the *Camino Reales* in Texas and California. The Old Spanish Trail differed from the others, however, in that it had been a slave route. A few Indian tribes, such as the Utes, did business in slaves as early as the 1630's. The heaviest trade was with children, for they could be trained more easily to work in houses or mines. Most children sold to the Spaniards came from the Paiute tribes, although slave-dealing was later taken up by the Apaches.

The Old Spanish Trail started in Santa Fe and went northwest to a point near Salt Lake, Utah. From there, the trail proceeded southwest to Las Vegas, Nevada, and ended in San Gabriel, California. Before long, prospectors began using it to enter the area of Southern California and search for lost mines. Some stopped to work the mines at Santa Rita, New Mexico. These mines had not been worked since 1804. The story goes that the famous Jim Bowie nearly found the lost San Saba mine, but was stopped by an Indian attack. In 1828 some new mines called the Placeres were started south of Santa Fe. This find brought a new rush of prospectors, who turned westward into Arizona, seeking the mines that had been deserted by the missionaries and the Spaniards nearly two centuries before.

In California the group that had the greatest influence were neither settlers nor trappers but the traders who came by ship. California had already attracted the British and the Russians and to some degree the Yankee captains from Boston. The combination of Mexican independence and the opening up of trade with the United States attracted more of the Clipper ships. They brought cotton goods and hardware to California and traded these items for otter and beaver skins. Sailing on to China, they traded the furs for silk and tea. Once home in Boston harbor they sold their cargo at a profit of from ten to twenty percent. Some Clipper ships on the way to China would load up not only with furs but also with tallow and hides. They would take a short run to Mexico, Peru or Chile where they would get rid of the tallow. The hides were kept aboard to sell in New England to the growing boot and shoe industry.

Monterey was becoming a busy port. Soon several firms from various parts of the world had established their branches there. When trading company representatives announced the expected arrival of a ship, people from outlying areas would flock into Monterey, many of them crowding aboard to shop for the goods that were laid out on display.

Some of the traders began to enlarge their interests and to seek permanent settlement in California. Mexican law required a foreigner who wanted to buy land to become a Mexican citizen and to convert to the Catholic religion. Many did as the law required, while others married Mexican women, acquiring land as a part of the wife's dowry. Still others simply got around the requirements in various ways.

A few of these traders developed huge businesses. For example, John Sutter, a Swiss American, received permission from Governor Alvarado in 1840 to develop a ranch in the Sacramento Valley. The ranch became known as New Helvetia. The next year Sutter bought Fort Ross from the Russians. The fort grew as an important trading center, and Sutter became a very wealthy man.

The first Anglo American settlers to come to California as a group arrived in 1841. The group was organized by John Bidwell, a school teacher, who was so inspired by reports of California that he organized the Western Emigration Society. His party of 69 people left Missouri, following the Platte River and then crossing over to Salt Lake. There they picked up a trail that had been opened up by the trapper William Walker and made their way to the San Joaquin Valley. Mexican officials arrested these illegal immigrants but soon released them, permitting them to settle wherever they wished in California. By 1842, there were about 475 foreigners and 2,200 Mexicans living in California.

Other Anglo American settlers began moving into California. Some came from New Mexico by way of the Old Spanish Trail. Some came in groups, others in small parties. By 1846, the Anglo American population numbered nearly 1,000. Many of the adventurous travelers went through terrible experiences on the way west for they had to cross the deserts or climb the Sierras to reach their destination. The famous ordeal of the Donner Party has been the subject of many books. The party of 79, trapped in the Sierras in mid-winter, numbered only 45 by the time it was rescued.

Despite such hardships, the stream of Anglo Americans continued. It did not take them long to adopt the life style of the Mexicans. They found the relaxed pace of life to be pleasant. They liked the Mexican manner of allowing time for interests other than those involving business. They learned how to raise cattle. They found out which crops grew best and mastered the tricks of irrigation.

Meanwhile, the Mexican learned from the Anglo Americans ways of handling business. Here the Anglo's practical nature and know-how proved to be to his advantage. The Mexicans began to need and seek those products made by the factories of New England. They appreciated the high quality of manufactured goods such as guns, nails, ploughs, shoes, and so forth. Even though transportation costs made these items very expensive, the Mexicans grew to depend on them.

In *Tejas*, where the foreigners outnumbered the Mexicans, Anglo Americans threatened the existing way of life. They demanded changes in government and social organizations. They wanted the way of life more in keeping with what they understood best.

Mounting Pressure for Statehood

From asking for changes in the system it was but one step more for Anglo Americans to think about changing *Tejas* from a territory to the status of state in the Republic of Mexico. To them the idea seemed simple; to the Mexican government it involved complicated matters. As a state, *Tejas* would become too autonomous. It might even consider declaring its independence. Mexico had to strengthen itself against the mounting pressure of the "Manifest Destiny" of the United States. *Tejas* served Mexico as a buffer.

"Manifest Destiny" is a term with many meanings. The one most generally accepted refers to the belief by leaders of the United States during the 1800's that the United States system of government and way of life were best for all people. Their belief in this concept extended beyond existing borders of their own country. They argued that people should be made "free" in order to enjoy the American way of life. With this philosophy went the belief that the United States should extend its natural boundaries from ocean to ocean. One congressman in Washington, D.C., expressed it this way:

> "The great engineer of the universe has fixed the natural limits of our country, and man cannot change them. That at least is above the treaty making power. To that boundary we shall go; peaceably if we can, forcibly if we must."

But Mexico had its own version of "manifest destiny," which was not based on extending itself beyond its borders, but on establishing at last a government and way of life that recognized the contributions of all of its people. Mexico had fought for independence for many of the same reasons and ideals as had the Thirteen Colonies. Mexico had written a constitution, the Constitution of 1824, much like that of the United States. Its government was organized along the same lines. Yet Mexico lacked one very important thing: experience in self-government.

This lack of experience made Mexico's government very unstable. Up to the time of the war for independence the important offices in government had been filled by Spaniards, giving the *criollos* and the *mestizos* little chance to be involved in decision-making. This inequality was in fact one of the causes for the war. Now that *criollos* and *mestizos* held in their hands the responsibility for governing, their lack of experience showed. It led to weak leadership. Leaders changed often.

The changes were not always smooth; many times they were accompanied by revolutions. These constant upheavals in Mexico's government upset the Texans (the new name for both Anglo Americans and Mexicans) who wanted Texas to become a state. Adding to their discontent, Mexico passed a law in 1829 that did away with slavery. Many of the Anglo American settlers from the South had brought their slaves with them and these Texans protested angrily against the law which would destroy their livelihoods. In response to their protests, the Mexican government had second thoughts; perhaps it would be best to make Texas an exception and allow Texans to keep their slaves. But the Texans remained wary and uncertain. This kind of law-making was not to their liking. Mexico, receiving persistent offers from the United States for the sale of its northern lands, was becoming annoyed and fearful. Mexican leaders complained that it had been a mistake to admit Anglo American settlers in the first place.

A study was authorized by the Mexican government requesting General Manuel Mier y Teran to determine how much of a threat the Anglos presented. The general reported that Texas was indeed headed for trouble. The Anglo American colonists were seeking to break Texas away from Mexico and add it to the United States. As a result, a law was passed in April 1830, closing Texas to any more Anglo American settlers, except those going to the Austin colonies. The same law also stopped the *impresario* grants and the importation of Black slaves and further placed a heavy tax on all imports coming into Texas. To make sure the law was carried out, 1,800 Mexican soldiers were sent to Texas. The government also encouraged Mexicans to settle there by giving them land grants taken back from the Anglo Americans. Needless to say, these developments angered the Anglo Americans.

Anglo discontent led to a new series of attempts to secure Mexican statehood for Texas. Each attempt ended in failure. The government of Mexico meanwhile continued its uncertain ways and showed little concern for the frustrated Anglo American colonists in faraway Texas. Finally, Texans were granted certain rights, including their own supreme court, trial by jury and permission to use English in official business.

But the Texans were still not satisfied; talk favoring complete independence was beginning to be heard everywhere. One of the spokesmen was Sam Houston, a close friend of President Andrew Jackson. Houston had come to Texas by way of the Cherokee lands and was the adopted son of a Cherokee chief. He had lived as a young man with the Indians and had been a soldier with Jackson in the War of 1812. His political background included the governorship of Tennessee. An unhappy marriage had sent him back to the wilderness. One day he appeared in Texas in the company of James Bowie. Houston joined the group of Texans who wanted to make Texas independent and was soon accepted as their leader.

A sudden change in the Mexican government brought the situation in Texas to the boiling point. In 1833 Antonio Lopez de Santa Anna had become head of the Mexican government. More dictator than president, Santa Anna in one year did away with the Constitution of 1824. He reorganized Mexico by breaking up all states and dividing the country into six sections, or departments. With this act he swept away the Texas plan for statehood.

Santa Anna knew that the Texans would object. To guarantee his control of Texas he sent an army under his brother-in-law to protect the frontiers and collect taxes. All Texans reacted with anger to this move. When the army arrived in the fall of 1835, the settlers banded together, fought the Mexican soldiers at Gonzales, a town near San Antonio, and forced them out of Texas.

Santa Anna simply sent back a larger army, which this time marched in and took over San Antonio on October 27, 1835. They made El Alamo, the old mission chapel, into a fort.

Other Texans organized and planned for war. At this point they were concerned not with complete independence but for the return of the Constitution of 1824. Both the Mexicans and the Anglo Americans wanted their natural rights as men living in a free country. On October 15, 1835, at Washington-on-the-Brazos they met to organize a government. Henry Smith was named governor and Sam Houston commander of the army. Stephen Austin and two others went to Washington, D.C., seeking help from the United States.

Under Sam Houston the army of Texas marched westward to San Antonio, growing as it moved. On December 5, 1835, the Texans attacked. After a four-day battle the Mexican army was defeated at San Antonio and was again forced out of Texas.

Once the battle was over most Texans returned to their homes. But Sam Houston was not finished. He moved south with a small army, hoping to start a general revolt against Santa Anna. Messengers soon caught up with Houston and reported that another army of Mexicans was crossing into Texas at Matamoros, this one led by Santa Anna himself. He was also told that the Texas government was falling apart. Houston turned his army eastward toward Washington-on-the-Brazos and sent Bowie back to San Antonio with orders to destroy the fort of the Alamo.

In San Antonio, Bowie met David Crockett and a band of volunteers. They decided that instead of destroying the Alamo they would defend it, even though Santa Anna's army was reported to be vastly larger than their own group.

At Washington-on-the-Brazos the declaration of independence from Mexico was written and signed on March 2, 1836. Texas was renamed the Lone Star Republic, a constitution was formed and David G. Burnet was elected president, with Lorenzo de Zavala vice president.

Meanwhile Santa Anna reached San Antonio, and on February 23, 1836, he attacked the Alamo. Inside the fort were 180 men armed with long rifles that had a range of 200 yards. The defenders also had twenty-one large guns. Facing them in attack was Santa Anna's army of 2,400 men. Most of them were Mayan Indian conscripts (men forced into the army) who did not speak Spanish and were unskilled with firearms. They were equipped with rifles with a range of only 70 yards. In addition, the army had eight or ten large guns. The defenders inside held off for twelve days, but on March 6 the Alamo fell. Nearly everyone in it was killed.

Many stories and myths have come out of this famous battle. Most of them pay no attention to the fact that only about 60 of those in the Alamo were Texans. The rest were recently arrived Anglo American adventurers. Nor does history remember the Mexicans who died in the Alamo fighting for Texas independence. The stories are not clear about other points of history, either. Few note that at the time Texas was a part of Mexico. Not until ten years after the battle did it become a part of the United States.

Other Battles

Soon after the Alamo, another battle took place on March 27 near Goliad. The Texan army of 400 men was completely destroyed, for Santa Anna had refused to take prisoners. The war in Texas was still not over; the final battle was to take place at the San Jacinto River.

After the battle at Goliad, Santa Anna started eastward to capture Houston. Houston retreated, drawing Santa Anna and his army of conscripts far from their lines of supply. On April 20, Houston stopped at the San Jacinto River. The next day he attacked, taking the Mexican army completely by surprise. The tired, frightened Indian conscripts ran into the swamps where six hundred were killed, many having no guns or swords to defend themselves. Santa Anna was captured. To save himself he granted the Lone Star Republic its freedom.

The Mexican government refused to recognize Texas independence and rejected Santa Anna as its true leader. As far as the Texans were concerned, the war was over. They were free and independent.

This was the first of a series of events that would see Mexico lose its great territories in the north.

6

The Southwest

PART I — WAR WITH THE UNITED STATES

Between 1845 and 1853 the United States acquired from Mexico the present states of Texas, New Mexico, Arizona, California, Nevada, Utah, and parts of Wyoming, Colorado, Kansas, and Oklahoma. To understand Mexico's sale of her northern territories, it is necessary to review the causes for the war with the United States.

Causes for War

After the Texas War and the defeat of Santa Anna at the San Jacinto River there were hard feelings between Mexico and the United States. Mexico accused the United States of backing the Texas rebels. Some Mexicans even charged that the whole war had been an American plan. The United States denied this charge, giving as proof that it had not added Texas to the Union. Yet the United States was the first nation to recognize Texas as an independent country. This was evidence enough for Mexico that the United States had indeed played a part. The government of Mexico warned the United States that if Texas was annexed, it would mean war between the two countries.

Another cause involved a claim of $2,000,000 against the Mexican government by a group of American citizens who had property and investments in different parts of Mexico. They claimed that during the many violent changes of Mexican government they had suffered heavy losses. Mexico was willing to settle, but while it made three payments on the debt, it could not make the last one. The United States considered this failure to be a lack of honor on the part of Mexico.

Ill feeling between the two countries continued to grow. Many leaders in the United States government argued strongly for war. Indeed, these people were actually planning to start such a war.

Meanwhile, the United States was also eyeing California, especially after it learned that Great Britain was interested in acquiring it. If Great Britain were to get California, the United States could not achieve its "destiny" of extending from ocean to ocean.

Mexico was weak and knew it. It had been an independent country for only twenty years. Its many revolutions and changes of leadership had left it poor and disorganized in government and military strength.

Mexico considered its greatest military advantage to be the vast desert lands to the north. Unfortunately, these areas were not well populated and few troops were stationed there. Furthermore, most settlers in New Mexico and California were very independent. They had learned long before not to count on the government to solve their problems. New Mexicans had protected themselves for years against the constant Indian raids. In 1841 they had withstood alone an invasion by Texas. People in New Mexico considered themselves New Mexicans first and Mexicans second. For many similar reasons, the California settlers thought of themselves as *Californios* rather than Mexicans.

In February 1845, the United States Congress voted in favor of annexation of Texas. In an angry response, Mexico broke off its relations with the United States. She had not yet even officially recognized Texas as an independent country and was about to make that move. Mexico wanted to put an end to the constant "border wars" and the angry disputes between settlers on either side of the border over property rights. These little battles had created long-lasting feelings of suspicion, fear and hatred between Mexicans and Texans. The American vote for annexation came at a wrong time for Mexico. With Texas now a state, the United States would become directly involved in the border war. In fact, the United States would be responsible.

During and after the annexation of Texas, the United States continued to make offers for the northern lands. Mexico continued to turn the offers down. In the fall of 1845, President Polk of the United States made a final bid of $25,000,000 for California up to and including San Francisco Bay. Part of this money would cover Mexico's debt to the United States. Mexico, at that time facing new problems of little money and uncertain leadership, still refused Polk's "final offer."

From the beginning of his term in office, President Polk gave the impression that he could not understand Mexico's point of view. First, he did not comprehend Mexico's reaction to Texas and its independence. Second, he failed to see why Mexico resented the United States' vote to annex that territory. Most of all, Polk and his supporters could not figure out why Mexico should refuse to sell a portion of its territory over which it had no control.

But it was a question of honor, not money. No Mexican, whether in Aztlán or the heart of Mexico, would accept having a foreigner settle his debts. Nor would a Mexican allow a foreigner to buy his land without regard for his *mejicano* brothers who lived on it. To Mexicans, the offer was an insult.

The Mexican rejection stung the United States into action. President Polk ordered all ports of Mexico to be blockaded. His excuse was that Mexico would now pay the money it owed to United States citizens. The blockade was followed by military action on both sides. While the United States called for volunteers to join the army, Mexico sent troops to reinforce its borders.

Territories Annexed

Meanwhile the Republic of Texas accepted the United States offer for annexation in June, 1845, and on December 29 of that year, Texas was made the 28th state of the Union. Immediately the United States sent troops to protect its border.

No one knows who started the fight on April 25, 1846 between American and Mexican soldiers at the Rio Grande near Matamoros. During the fight, the American soldiers were captured. President Polk, upon hearing this news, sent a message to Congress asking for a declaration of war. In his message, Polk made a point of saying that Mexico had struck the first blow. The truth was not known then, nor is it known today. Nevertheless, Congress went along with his request. Two years of war followed.

The length of the war was surprising considering Mexico's weakness. Some important factors helped her continue the fight. One was the considerable distance between any major American community and Mexico's heart, Mexico City. Another was that in 1845, warfare was a slow process. It took a long time to move an army and keep it supplied. A third point in Mexico's favor was that the United States was an invading army.

The United States invaded Mexico from four different directions. One army entered northern Mexico across the Rio Grande. A second went overland through New Mexico and Arizona to California. A third was transported by sea to the California ports. The fourth landed at Gulf of Mexico ports and marched over the mountains to Mexico City. (See map.) No part of the war was fought on United States soil.

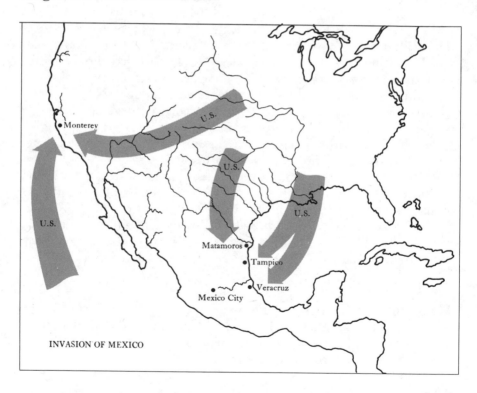

INVASION OF MEXICO

The United States calls it the Mexican War, but in Mexico it is known as the War with the United States. Not all Americans supported the war. Many northerners called it unjust and argued that it was forced upon a weak neighbor in order to steal territory to form slave states. Still others called it a "black spot" on the American flag. American newspapers carried reports of outrages and atrocities committed by American troops, many of them undisciplined volunteers. By most reports, these men were a disgrace to the American flag. General Winfield Scott, who led the army into Mexico City, admitted that his soldiers had "committed atrocities to make Heaven weep and every American of Christian morals blush for his country."

Some actions of the war were accomplished easily. When Colonel Stephen Watts Kearny entered Santa Fe, he met no resistance. Here are parts of two letters written by an American soldier:

"... Some few of the Mexican citizens prompted by curiosity, came out in their white shirts and wide breeches, with those everlasting hats on, and looked with gaping wonder, on the advanced corps of the 'Army of the West.' ... Horses went to sleep hungry, for not a spear of grass was in sight, and men wondered what would come next . . . and speculated on the price of bread and cards in Santa Fe.

At length the artillery appeared—the bugle call to horse, and into the town we marched, with drawn sabres, and taking as much care of the little urchins in the streets as we would on parade in St. Louis—and, by the way children are everywhere the same, when soldiers or any other show are on the tapis. The General took his position with his guard in the plaza or great square before the palace, where he claimed the capital and country of the alcalde for the American Union, and administered the oath of allegiance, while Major Sumner marched us through several streets, and the American flag was hoisted over the palace, saluted by the deep voices of Major Clark's artillery from the hill where we had halted. We were then marched out to the hill again, where we found that the wagons of our company had not come up, and that the prospect for supper was no longer dubious, but decidedly bad; while our poor horses, tired beyond measure, had no chance of a single blade to stand between themselves and starvation.
Well—supper or not—here we are in Santa Fe—AND NEW MEXICO IS OURS!"

"Our march into the city, as I have told you, was extremely warlike, with drawn sabres, and daggers in every look. From around corners, men with surly countenances and downcast looks regarded us with watchfulness, if not terror; and black eyes looked through latticed windows at our column of cavaliers, some gleaming with pleasure, and others filled with tears. Strange indeed, must have been the feelings of the citizens when an invading army was thus entering their home— themselves used only to look on soldiers as plagues sent to eat out their substance, burn, ravage and destroy—all the future of their destiny vague and uncertain—their new rulers strangers to their manners, language and habits, and, as they had been taught to believe, enemies to the only religion they had ever known. It was humiliating, too, to find their city thus entered, without a gun having been fired in its defence; and we thought that that humble, mortified pride was indicated in the expression of more than one swarthy face. As the American flag was raised, and the cannon boomed its glorious national salute from the hill, the pent-up emotions of many of the women could be suppressed no longer, and a sigh of commiseration, even for causeless distress, escaped from many a manly breast, as the wail of grief arose above the din of our horses' tread, and reached our ears from the depth of the gloomy-looking buildings on every hand."

Most reports have said the taking of New Mexico was bloodless, but the story of its conquest is not a serene one. The truth is that the Mexicans hated their conquerors. The Indians, at first indifferent, soon wished for the return of Mexican rule. A number of incidents brought unrest and sorrow to Mexicans and Pueblos. Several plots to get rid of the *americanos* were led by high-ranking New Mexicans, priests and Pueblos. At Taos on January 19, 1847, several of these Mexicans and Pueblos united to revolt against the *americanos*. In the fighting, a Mexican who sided with *americanos* was killed, as well as other *americanos*. Included was Governor Charles Bent, even though he had a Mexican wife. Some men were scalped alive, then tortured to death. Another incident at Las Vegas resulted in serious fighting and many deaths. The Indians of Mora destroyed their own pueblo and fled to the hills rather than to give in to the invaders.

In California, the leadership situation made it possible for the United States to take over the territory with little effort. For a long time California had gone its own separate way from Mexico. The 2,000 miles between the Mexican capital and Monterey prevented any regular contact or control. Close to the hearts of many of the rich *Californios* was the dream of making California an independent country. But the dream was not to be realized, for they could not agree on the man to lead them.

The choice, over which the *Californios* disagreed violently, was between José Castro in northern California and Pio Pico in southern California. Into this crisis stepped John C. Fremont, an officer in the United States Army. Fremont had previously "explored" California as a civilian on four separate occasions, traveling with trappers and guides. From his experiences Fremont, with his wife's help, wrote and published reports about California that became popular reading in the eastern United States. People fondly nicknamed him "Pathfinder of the West."

On his fifth "exploration" expedition, in 1846, John C. Fremont brought along officials from the United States government and heavy military equipment. The party entered California across the Rockies by way of Utah. After making a stop at Sutter's Fort near Sacramento, the "Pathfinder" and his 62 companions continued their "scientific" progress toward the coast. They were now in violation of the permission granted them by the Mexican government and were ordered out of California. As the party marched northward, they were met by an agent of the United States. Fremont's written account tells that the agent brought news of the coming war between Mexico and the United States. The agent also reportedly brought orders from President Polk for Fremont to win over the *Californios* to the side of the United States. So Fremont turned back, determined to study carefully the situation among the *Californios*.

He soon found himself in the midst of a group of fellow Anglo Americans who were worried about their fate in case of civil war between northern and southern California. Fremont advised them what course of action to follow.

The first move was made by Ezekeil Merritt and thirty-four other settlers. They took over the *presidio* at Sonoma and arrested eighteen Mexicans, among them Mariano Vallejo, founder of the settlement at Sonoma. Then, on June 14, 1846, William B. Ide led the Anglo American settlers in proclaiming California independent. They created their own flag, a grizzly bear standing against a white background. They called the new country the Bear Flag Republic.

On July 2, 1846, a troopship of the United States Navy sailed into the harbor at Monterey. Five days later troops debarked and took possession of the town. Upon hearing this, Fremont assumed leadership in Sonoma. Another United States warship captured San Francisco and dispatched troops to Sonoma. There, the soldiers pulled down the Bear Flag and raised the Stars and Stripes, taking possession of northern California for the United States.

The war in northern California was over, but the conquest of southern California was to prove not such a simple matter.

On August 13, 1846, the Army of the United States entered Los Angeles and four days later issued a proclamation that,

> "The Flag of the United States is now flying from every commanding position in the Territory, and California is free from Mexican dominion."

This was followed by an order of martial law, which meant that all existing laws ended, with the Army alone in control.

Everything was quiet for a few days. Satisfied, the army withdrew, leaving behind a small body of troops. Within a short time, these *gringos* (as the Anglo Americans were called) learned of their unpopularity with the residents. When an officer attempted to arrest a Mexican, the people quickly rose up against the troops. The soldiers were forced to retreat to their base, Fort Hill. The fort, built on a hill behind the *plaza,* offered a view of the whole town but was without a source of fresh water.

Meanwhile, a skirmish took place on an outlying ranch in which the Anglo Americans were defeated. Filled with excitement over this victory, the Mexicans tightened their encirclement of Fort Hill. The troops within the fort, without water or food, were finally forced to surrender to the people of Los Angeles. The soldiers were allowed to go to the port of San Pedro, hopefully to board a ship and leave.

But one messenger had managed to escape the fort during the siege. This man, Juan Flaco Brown, rode to San Francisco for help, covering the distance of 500 miles in five days. The help summoned by Brown arrived before the American ship left San Pedro, and the two American forces joined to recapture Los Angeles.

The Battle of Rancho Dominguez followed. Here, the united *gringos* met an unexpectedly strong troop of Mexicans. They were astounded at the skill of the Mexican horsemen. The Mexicans, armed with poor guns and willow lances, were more than the *gringos* could handle. The Mexicans offered still another surprise, a small cannon that had been hidden from the *gringos* by a Mexican woman. They mounted it on a wagon and moved it about, firing on the American soldiers from all directions. The Americans wore themselves out trying to capture the gun, and finally gave up and withdrew in defeat.

However, two more American forces were closing in on Los Angeles. One, led by John C. Fremont, came from Monterey. The other marched up from the south with General Kearny as leader and Kit Carson as guide. On November 25, after a two-month desert crossing, they entered California. Once there, Kearny's army engaged in battle with the *Californios* led by Andrés Pico, cousin of Pio Pico. At the Battle of San Pascual, sixteen American soldiers were killed and many were wounded, while the Mexicans suffered only minor casualties.

Unfortunately for the Mexicans, Kit Carson and a companion sneaked past their sentries and made it to the coast. There they secured help from the American warships anchored at San Diego. Carson returned to General Kearny at San Pascual with an escort of 200 marines and soldiers. At the sight of this large force, the Mexicans drew back, and General Kearny swept on to San Diego, claiming victory over the *Californios*.

Not until January of 1847 did Kearny and his army move toward Los Angeles. Small companies of Mexicans delayed them on their way, but they were civilians, neither organized nor trained for warfare, and could not really stop the advancing army. On January 10, 1847, Los Angeles was occupied by the Army of the United States.

The final battle to win California involved Fremont's troops. On January 13, 1847 he and his 400 riflemen reached Cahuenga Pass, near Los Angeles. There they met forces led by Andrés Pico. Heavily outnumbered, Pico surrendered to Fremont. The signing of the Treaty of Cahuenga Pass brought to an end the fighting in California between the Mexicans and their conquerors.

The Californios

The details of this section of the war point up the character of the *Californio*. The *Californio* was a strong individual, rough and tough. He dearly loved his way of life and made every effort to defend it against the invader. The real way of the *Californio* has been somehow changed into a romantic style. Mention has been made earlier of mistaken ideas of the *Californio* and his way of life as shown in literature and the media.

California had a social structure similar to that of New Mexico. The great differences were found in the number of people in each territory and the way these people made a living. California had a small population. The main industry was cattle. Cattle was raised for hides and fat. A man's wealth was measured not by the size of his land holdings but by the size of his stock of cattle. Land was easy to come by. Most *Californios* owned hundreds of acres of land. Land was essential for cattle raising, for the herds required vast grazing areas. As a matter of fact, the great herds of wild horses had to be hunted down to make room for the cattle.

This type of industry in California made for a pastoral life. That is to say, life was quiet and fairly simple. The set patterns of living rarely varied. There was little regard for money. Business was generally done by bartering or trading. The pastoral life allows time for many amusements. Most entertainment was connected in some way with the raising of cattle. For instance, out of the need to protect the cattle from killers came the bear hunt. Hunting the grizzly bear with *lasso* became a very popular sport. The necessity to thin down the wild horse herds invented other thrilling kinds of sport. To capture the *mestengo* (mustang) tested the ability of a man to handle the *lasso* and to break the wild horse. The *rodeo* (round up) offered the chance for entire communities to gather together for gala occasions. At the *rodeo* men could talk over the ownership of lands. This business was a verbal agreement, for there were no fences as boundaries. All land was open range.

The *Californios* enjoyed such spectacles as bull and bear fights, cockfights and horse racing. Of course dancing was always a pleasure, especially the *fandango*. Any occasion made good reason for *fiesta* or great party: the birth of a baby, a marriage, a saint's day and so forth.

The *Californios* had developed a style of dress well adapted to their work. Some features of this dress were common to most Southwestern peoples. But the *Californios* added their special touch. The trousers had huge flares, beginning at the knee, to allow room for the boots and out-size spurs. They used gold and silver thread to decorate their clothing. They wore blouses and shirts made of luxurious silk and velvet. The *Californios,* involved with trade from the Orient, showed their easy access to exotic materials.

The women generally dressed in keeping with the fashion of the times. Like the men, they took full advantage of the chance to use materials not common to all Mexican colonists. In the home, they capably managed their households and arranged for the constant entertainment of their day. Outside the home, women often rode horseback and hunted along with men.

Californios were everywhere famous for their hospitality. Rarely was any traveler turned away from a hearty welcome. Lodging, meals and fresh horses were freely given. At times, guests were even given extra money to help them along their way.

The above description deals mainly with the landowning people of California. These *Californios* were the *Dons*.

The people who owned no property were members of the lower classes. These lower classes included the soldiers, *peons* and Indian servants. California became the new home for many former convicts from Mexico. These convicts had been given the choice of prison or colonizing the far-off territory. (Many mother countries followed this practice. The colony of Georgia was settled by former convicts from England.) To the established settlers of California, the "convict settlers" became an unfortunate problem. The *Californios* called them *cholos* (scoundrels). In some cases the *cholos* would band together and continue their life of crime or anti-social behavior.

Primarily, the pastoral life in California remained a settler's life. It was hard and demanding, as pioneer life always has been. Their every need had to be provided for from scratch. They themselves were responsible for all they owned and produced. As a result, they became very independent. They also became proud. To feel put upon was open invitation for them to fight.

Present day movies and T.V. serials tend to show the people of early California living in great houses or luxurious *ranchos*. These mistakes arise from movie makers' fantasies, induced by such novels as *Ramona* by Helen Hunt Jackson. The Mexican settlers of California lived comfortably, it is true. But their homes were small and modest, as can be seen by visits to present day remains. The report that follows gives the contemporary view of such a Mexican home. J. E. Pleasants, when a school boy of sixteen, visited the home of Andrés Pico soon after the war. Young Pleasants wrote in a composition for his teacher what he saw as a typical day in the life of a *Californio*:

"... Like the grandee that he (Pico) was, he entertained lavishly. His silver and china table service made a brilliant display. His household furnishings were plain but massive ... The plain old mission furniture was retained but many an expensive and more ornate piece had been added. His table afforded an ample style of living; the dinners consisted of five to six courses—all of the far-famed California-Spanish cookery, which no nation—not even the French, has ever excelled. Two young Indian boys served as waiters. They were clad in the simple tunic of the day. Before the meal, one them stood by the host, *Don* Andrés, at the head of the table and said grace, and at the close of the meal, the other took his place and returned thanks. At the mid-day and evening meals, and on the veranda in the evening, we were delightfully entertained by native musicians who played on three stringed instruments then mostly in vogue—the harp, violin and guitar. They played the dreamy old Spanish airs which were to me, the most enjoyable feature of the day which, with the long rides after stock on a spirited horse, was, in itself, all that the heart of a western boy could desire. After the noon dinner, all work was suspended for the customary two hour siesta. The cool rooms of the thick-walled adobe afforded a refreshing change from the July sunshine of the open plains, and the siesta was a welcome interval after a strenuous morning's work, for we were all out on the range before the sun was well over the Tujunga peaks ... the General took good care of the building and the orchards during his occupancy, and he surely knew how to entertain his friend and his pupils."

Arizona offered little resistance to the invader. Its main community, Tucson, fell without a shot being fired. Yet the story of its capture is fascinating.

At the time of the war the Mormons, a religious group, were seeking settlement in the far West, mainly to avoid the persecution they suffered in the East. Their leader, Brigham Young, proposed to the United States government that he put together a fighting force, the Mormon Battalion, to help with the invasion of the northern lands. In return, the army was to aid in the westward transfer of his people.

The army at first rejected Young's proposal, but later relented in part, agreeing that four families could accompany the battalion. On July 21, 1846, the group set out from Nauvoo, Illinois, under the command of Captain James Allen, who was a military man but not a Mormon. Nearly three months later, on October 9, they arrived in Santa Fe. The march had proved an ordeal, with many lives lost along the way.

After a ten-day rest, they pushed on for their destination, San Diego, about 600 miles away. On this leg of their journey, the desert sands cut their progress to 12 miles a day and added to their casualties through starvation, thirst, exhaustion, and death. Written accounts by some of the Mormons also tell of attacks by fierce wild bulls left behind by Mexican settlers fleeing from the Apaches.

Tucson, the only Mexican stronghold in Arizona, numbered 500 people. The settlement itself consisted of about twenty adobe buildings, an arsenal and an army barracks. The town was protected by thick adobe walls, but the Mexican soldiers were poorly prepared to defend it. When the Mormon Battalion arrived, the Mexicans withdrew without a fight. The battalion stayed in Tucson for only one day before pushing on for San Diego.

Finally, on January 28, 1847, they reached the Pacific Ocean. Besides capturing Tucson, the Mormon Battalion had accomplished another goal. They had succeeded in making a trail between Santa Fe and San Diego which would become one of the most important gateways to California. Most of the men then sent for their families and settled in California near the town of San Bernardino.

By February 1847, all of Mexico's northern territories were under the control of United States forces. In the months that followed General Winfield Scott marched his troops west from Vera Cruz, Mexico and, after a number of terrible battles in which both sides suffered heavy losses, took Mexico City itself.

The Treaty of Guadalupe Hidalgo

On February 2, 1848, the Treaty of Guadalupe Hidalgo was signed. According to the treaty Mexico recognized Texas as being part of the United States. For $15,000,000 it sold the occupied borderlands of New Mexico, Arizona and California. The boundary between Mexico and the United States was set from El Paso

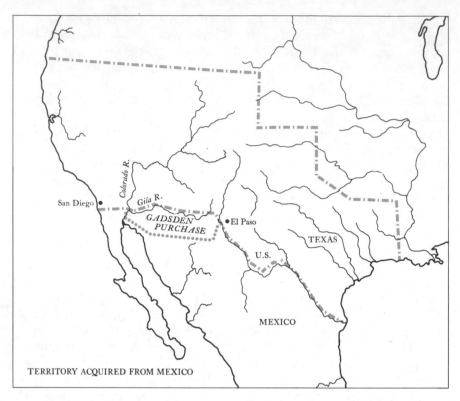

San Diego

Colorado R.

Gila R.

GADSDEN PURCHASE

El Paso

TEXAS

U.S.

MEXICO

TERRITORY ACQUIRED FROM MEXICO

on the Rio Grande to the Continental Divide, then northward to the Gila River. The line followed the Colorado River to its mouth, continuing straight westward across California to a point one league (4.6 miles) south of San Diego on the coast. (See map.)

Mexicans living north of the boundary were given the choice of remaining in their homes or moving to Mexico. Those who chose the latter were granted land by the Mexican government. Approximately 2,000 people returned. Those who chose to stay were granted full rights of citizenship as stated in the United States Constitution. The treaty also guaranteed to respect all land grants made by the Mexican government. No personal rights were guaranteed to the Indians for both governments looked upon them as savages. The United States government agreed to keep "the savages" under control but promised "special care" that no Indian would be forced to leave his home. This first provision took into account the fact that Indian tribes went on the warpath when their lands were invaded.

Many of the terms of the treaty almost copied the offers of purchase the United States had made before the war. Some historians have concluded that men in power provoked the war in order to force Mexico to sell its northern territories. This conclusion has received new emphasis in light of contemporary activities of the Mexican Americans. The major immediate effects of the treaty were to increase the size of the United States by more than one-third and to fulfill the country's "manifest destiny," by extending from ocean to ocean. The events that followed the signing of the treaty placed greater emphasis on the territorial gains than on the rights of the new American citizens.

Even before the signing of the treaty, an incident occurred in California which was to throw the United States into wild excitement. Gold was discovered! Why had the Spaniards and Mexicans not found it? After all, had they not been the daring explorers? Were they not skillful miners? There are good reasons. First, the Mexicans had limited their settlements to the coast, bypassing the interior areas. Second, the Indians had shown no signs of possessing gold. Third, the *Californios* seemed happy enough with their pastoral life. And fourth, of course, is plain bad luck.

E. L. Cleveland, an enthusiastic supporter of "manifest destiny," provided the answer:

> "Why sir, did God preserve this whole country . . . ? In fine, why were the immense treasures of California hidden from the world until she was annexed to this Republic? And tell me, if anyone can, why it was the title of transference had no sooner passed into our hands, than she gave up her mighty secret and unlocked her golden gates?"

This attitude was shared by a number of Anglo American gold seekers, who felt that providence had chosen them especially to enjoy the wealth of California. As "favored" people, they considered anyone unlike themselves to be outsiders and inferiors.

The Gold Rush

The finding of gold in California is a familiar story. On January 24, 1848, while building a sawmill at Coloma on the present American River, James Marshall came across nuggets of gold. This discovery created a boom that brought immigrants by the thousands to California.

Few people today realize that Marshall's find was not the first discovery of gold in California. On March 9, 1842, Francisco Lopez struck gold in Santa Feliciana Canyon, forty miles from Los Angeles, but the find received little notice because there were few settlers in the area. Mexicans had never given up the search for the gold that had pressed the *conquistadores* to explore the Southwest. For years Mexicans had been involved in mining enterprises. Previous chapters have given accounts of the early prospectors who had looked for the precious metal in New Mexico and Arizona. Some of the know-how they used in searching and digging they had learned from the various Indian nations. The Spanish miners had added these skills to the ones they already knew in the working of the mines of Spain.

According to the record, it was not "Gold!" that James Marshall shouted when he made his discovery at Sutter's ranch, but *"Chispa!"*, which is Spanish for spark, ember, sparkle. The word is commonly used by Mexican miners for gold. That James Marshall should use this term shows how widely the Mexican mining methods had spread.

When word of the gold spread in 1848, the *Californios* took off to the mountains. They had the advantage of being near the site of the discovery. One example of this activity is Don Antonio Cormel. Don Antonio, upon receiving the news, organized a group of thirty *Californios,* some newly arrived settlers from Sonora and some Indian servants. The group was lucky from the beginning. From some Indians who had nuggets they found out the source. In one day all of this happened: Don Antonio dug out forty-five ounces of gold; a woman in the group found a single twelve ounce nugget; a man gathered a towelful of nuggets from a boulder.

Don Antonio quickly sold his claim to one of the men who dug out fifty-two pounds of gold in eight days. In turn, nearly every member of the party struck it rich. Before long, well over 1,000 *Californios* took to the hunt for gold. The *Californios* did not work their diggings individually. They organized into groups. In this way, they worked over more ground and consequently found more gold.

The *Californios* held their peaceful advantage for about one year. With the arrival of Anglo American fortune hunters, conflicts began to develop. The Anglo Americans flatly shut out all foreigners from entering the gold fields. One conflict had such a serious outcome that a community was renamed Hangtown. Here, a Chilean and a Frenchman were hanged for reasons not too clear to anyone. Especially were the reasons unclear to the foreigners who were made to "dance on air."

Included as "foreigners" were former Mexicans who had become citizens of the United States under the Treaty of Guadalupe Hidalgo. The incidents of beatings and killings of non-Anglo Americans became more frequent. The Mexicans-turned-American citizens began to give up the search for gold. It was impossible to convince the *gringos* that they were fellow citizens sharing the same rights. In fact, the *Californios* began to be convinced that their bad thoughts about *gringos* were absolutely true. They could only agree when Hugo Reid described the people who had come to seek gold as:

> ". . . vagabonds from every quarter of the globe. Scoundrels from nowhere, rascals from Oregon, pick-pockets from New York, accomplished gentlemen from Europe, interlopers from Lima and Chile, Mexican thieves, gamblers of no particular spot, assassins manufactured in Hell for the express purpose of converting highways and byways into theatres of blood; then last but not least, Judge Lynch with his thousand arms, thousand sightless eyes and five-hundred lying tongues."

The *Californios* could easily believe that everything now wrong in California had come with the *gringo*. California had suffered an invasion of evil.

Before the discovery of gold, California had a population of hardly more than 15,000. Suddenly, in 1849, there were 100,000 newcomers. By 1852, there were 250,000 Californians. To add to the troubles of the original *Californios,* large numbers of Spanish-speaking people had emigrated from South America and Mexico. Without doubt, these adventurers were similar in character to the Anglo American gold-diggers. Without separating out the Spanish-speaking peoples, the Anglo Americans lumped them all together under the general term "greaser." As "greasers," the *Californios'* poor chances for equal citizenship with other Americans shrank to almost nothing.

Among the Mexicans who rushed to find California gold were thousands of miners from Sonora. The Sonora miners had been prevented by the Apaches from working their own mines in Sonora. (Sonora is the Mexican state that shares its border with Arizona and California.) They came in clusters of twenty or thirty families at a time. Most important, they brought their expert knowledge of how to extract the precious metal from the earth. The Anglo Americans lacked the know-how of mining for metal. Their mining in eastern United States had been limited to coal.

The Sonoran miners introduced the *batea* (pan) for creek bed or *placer* (sand bank) mining in California. They also showed the miners "dry digging," a process used where there is a shortage of water. With it, the mixture of gold and sand is dried over a fire or in the sun, then tossed into the air or fanned to separate the gold. This method was greatly used in the Southwest.

These Mexican miners were also the first to work the ore-rich quartz mines in California, where they used the *arrastre,* or "Chili Mill." The *arrastre* was a mill in the center of which was a pivot post. A mule hitched to the post dragged around a heavy piece of granite which crushed the quartz against a hard stone floor. The quartz was then pulled together by the use of mercury (quicksilver) and the gold or silver removed.

The use of quicksilver for separating silver or gold is called the *patio* process. (*Patio* refers to the stone floor.) It was invented in 1557 by Bartólome de Medina, a miner from Pachuca, Mexico. Captain Andrés Castillero, a young Mexican cavalry officer, discovered a rich quicksilver mine near San Jose, California in 1845. The mine was named *Nueva Almadén* (New Almaden) after the famous quicksilver mine in Spain. It has been said that without *Nueva Almadén,* the discovery of gold or silver would have meant very little.

Another important mine, the Comstock, near Virginia City, Nevada, was discovered by a Mexican, Ignacio Paredes from Alamos, Sonora. After Paredes abandoned it, Comstock, an Anglo American, came along and reopened the mine. He was looking for gold, but some "blue stuff" kept getting in the way. One day a Mexican miner came by while Comstock was working the *batea.* Noticing the "blue stuff," he became excited and shouted, *"Es plata! Hay mucha plata!"* ("It's silver! There's a lot of silver!") The Comstock mine became one of the richest silver mines of the world.

The contributions made by the Mexican to the mining industry of the Southwest can be partly measured by the number of Spanish words it commonly uses. Some examples are: *bonanza* (rich ore), *borrasco* (barren rock), *placer* (sandbank), *xacal* (slack), *escoria* (slag). The Mexican has also contributed to mining industry law. Anglo American miners who rushed to the Southwest during the great strikes found it best to adopt the legal system used by the Mexicans. These laws have formed the basis for mining industry regulations in the entire United States. Texas, in reserving a fifth of all profits from mining from 1836 to 1883 to establish a school system, was actually adopting the Spanish Crown's *quinta* system. As a matter of fact, the Southwestern states incorporated Mexican laws relative to other matters such as care of orphaned children, community property, riparian (water) rights, and so forth into their legal codes.

The techniques of copper mining were first developed in the Southwest after Apache Indians introduced the Spaniards and the Mexicans to the rich copper mines of Arizona. The Santa Rita mine was worked as early as 1800. Later other copper mines were discovered in Arizona in such places as Tubac and Bisbee, as well as in Utah and Nevada. It was Mexican labor and know-how that made these areas rich copper producers.

Out of the earth, the sand and the mountainsides the miners dug a fabulous wealth. It is estimated that the gold fields in Cali-

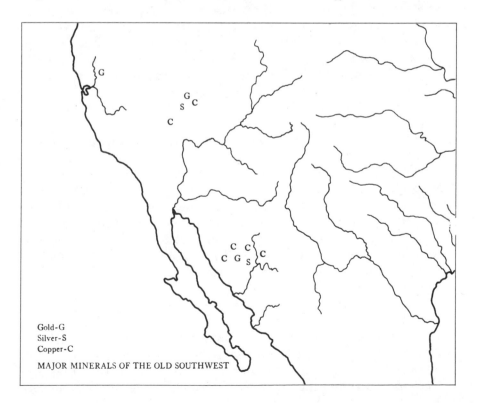

Gold-G
Silver-S
Copper-C

MAJOR MINERALS OF THE OLD SOUTHWEST

fornia alone produced $10,000,000 in 1849, $41,000,000 in 1850, and nearly $85,000,000 by 1852. The more wealth the mines produced, the many more thousands of people made their way to all parts of the Southwest, creating increased clashes between *gringos* and "greasers." Citizens of Mexican background had trouble functioning in a culture that daily grew more different from their own. As a cruel climax, the Californian began to feel like a foreigner in his own country. Even the land around him began to skyrocket in value as Anglo American speculators snapped it up. New clashes arose between Californians and Anglo Americans. And still the Americans kept coming.

A sudden demand for transportation developed for bringing in not only the immigrants, but also food and supplies. The first line of communication between the eastern states and California was a long ocean route, which involved a voyage around Cape Horn, the tip of South America. Soon ships were taking passengers to the Caribbean coast of Panama. Coaches rushed the passengers across the Isthmus of Panama to the Pacific Coast, where they sailed on to California.

Many immigrants made their way west on foot, breaking trails through lands where few white men had ever gone. Some travelers cut across Mexico creating problems of trespass that added to the tensions between the two countries. Within a short time there were overland mail and stage lines connecting East and West. California developed stage lines to transport people, goods and mail up and down the state and into the back country. By 1853 twelve busy stage lines were working in and out of Sacramento alone.

In the East, railroads were tying together various parts of the country, and people were beginning to talk about several railroad lines to span the entire width of the United States. The building of a southern railroad route along the boundary line as set in the Treaty of Guadalupe Hidalgo seemed unworkable. For one thing, trains would have to travel through extremely rough country. Furthermore, to stop at Tucson and Tubac, the most important towns in Arizona, the trains would have to enter Mexico. Mexico owned that strip as well as the Mesilla Valley, a nearby farmland northwest of El Paso.

In 1853, James Gadsden was sent to Mexico to see what he could do about acquiring this land for the United States. Santa Anna once again was in power and Mexico once again was short of funds. Gadsden was able to purchase the land, adding about 30,000 square miles to the United States for only $10,000,000. Mexican citizens who lived in the area were given the same choice as before. They could stay on their lands and become United States citizens or move into Mexico. Very few left. For the Apaches, the Gadsden Purchase proved a problem. No longer could they cross the border into Mexico after raiding American settlements. Most of the lands the Apaches had called their own was now United States territory.

PART II—THE CONQUEROR AND THE CONQUERED

To all of the Southwest Indians, the Gadsden Purchase and the changes that came with it had only one meaning. A new invader had entered their lands. The Comanches, the Navajos, and especially the Apaches resisted their new enemy as fiercely as they had the Mexican. Immediately, the American forces in New Mexico and Arizona found themselves face to face with the "Indian Menace" and built a series of forts whose names are familiar to us today mostly because of western movies. They include Fort Defiance, Fort Union, Fort Conrad, Fort Fillmore, Fort Webster, Fort Brecken-ridge, Fort Moore, Fort Buchanan and Fort Mojave. These forts served to protect the new settlers against the nomadic Indians who raided Pueblos, Mexicans and Anglo Americans alike. Attacks by the Apaches and the Navajos grew fiercer as the number of settlers increased. More and more clearly the Indians realized that they were being pushed off their lands. Some tribes, such as the Mojaves, were soon defeated and placed in reservations. But others refused to submit to such treatment. The Apaches were not farmers or growers of crops. They were not settlers or home-builders. They were hunters, a people constantly on the move in their search for food. Against the ever-advancing Anglos, they waged a nearly continuous war until 1866.

The Apaches

The Apaches were probably the most nomadic of all the South-west tribes. Their history goes back as far as 1000 A.D., a date which marks their departure from the Northwest tribes. Why they left is not known. From the northwest they migrated south, and by about 1550, they were moving down the western Great Plains. There they contacted the Zuñi Indians, who gave them the name "Apache," meaning enemy. As nomads, the Apaches relied on raiding as their means of food-getting. The Spanish introduction of cattle, horses and mules to the Southwest offered the Apaches their best sources for food.

There were six large divisions of Apaches, each with its own lands. The Kiowa-Apaches and the Lipans were on the plains. The Jicarillos and Mescaleros lived in New Mexico. The Western Apaches and Chiricahuas stayed in far west New Mexico and Arizona. Within these divisions were separate groups. The groups were not large, for most nomadic groups operate on a small scale. Each group managed its affairs independently of the others. They were like large families, with the chief acting mainly as adviser. Below the chiefs were sub-chiefs who generally ran the family. To be any type of chief, a man had to prove himself a superior hunter, warrior and speaker. The best warriors in each group were recognized as war chiefs. The war chiefs with other sub-chiefs controlled the ceremonies connected with war or raids. Sometimes, if an enemy was mighty, several groups would join as a war party. At such times, a single war chief was chosen as leader.

In their migration from the Northwest, the Apaches had picked up cultural features from the peoples they had contacted. Many of their myths and customs are like those of the Indians of the Northwest. Still others follow those of the Pueblos of the plains. Apaches do sand painting after the manner of the Pueblos. Like the Pueblos, they have a ceremonial rite in which men and women dance together. Only one group of Apaches adopted a life style of agriculture, the Western Apaches. They may have learned farming from the Navajos. Otherwise the Apaches were mainly gatherers and hunters.

The Apaches lived in dome shaped *wickiups*. The *wickiups* were built with mesquite, cottonwood, willow poles bound by yucca fiber and covered with brush and bear grass. In cold weather, the domes were covered with animal skins. In hot weather, the Apache people spent much of their time in the shade of *ramadas,* open-air shelters of brush and grass roofs resting upon poles.

Their clothing resembled that of the Pueblos. It was made of skins primarily. The men wore longsleeved shirts and breechcloths. The women dressed in two-piece outfits. Knee-high moccasins were common to men and women. The men's hair was long and unbraided, bound at the forehead with a leather band. Both men and women used earrings, necklaces, pendants and bracelets. Rarely were feathers part of their dress.

Apache women excelled at basket making. The baskets, black and brown in color, had geometric designs of animal or human forms. In addition to baskets the groups worked with tools such as fire drills, stone *manos* and *metates* (corngrinders), gourd cups and dishes, skin bags and pottery.

Although the Apache spread alarm as a raider, he was not really an expert horseman. He prized the horse mostly as food. When the Apaches raided or made war, they most often went by foot. Apaches learned to hate the white man soon after the Spanish invasion of Aztlán and Spanish settlers and missionaries suffered countless raids on their herds. In revenge, the Spanish offered money for their capture as slaves or for their scalps, a custom the Mexicans maintained. Many mountain men collected bounty money from Mexican officials in Chihuahua for Apache scalps. To a degree the Americans continued the practice.

An interesting sidelight is that the Treaty of Guadalupe Hidalgo recognized and condemned these practices. An entire section of the agreement deals with humane reforms regarding Indian slavery and trading with the "savage tribes."

The entrance of American troops into the newly acquired lands stirred up guerrilla warfare, which continued for nearly thirty-four years. This period saw the emergence of such famous Apache leaders as Mangas Coloradas, Cochise and Victorio.

Despite the promising words of the treaty, the Apaches were subject to abuse, mistreatment and injustice, some of it based on ignorance, much of it based on greed. The discovery of gold in Apache lands aggravated the bad feelings. In 1851, gold was found at Pinos Altos, the middle of Apache country. Within a few weeks, 140 gold-hungry American miners were digging away at the hills. The Apaches, led by the great Mangas Coloradas (Red Sleeves), at first tried to frighten away the *Pinda Lick-o-yi* (white eyes). But the attempt failed, for the *Pinda Lick-o-yi* would not be driven away. Their greed was greater than their fear. Mangas Coloradas said, "If it is gold that brought them here, it is gold that will get them out." Mangas Coloradas went alone to the miners, offering to direct them to some rich deposits. The miners, filled with distrust and bitterness, did not believe the Apache chief. They seized him, tied him to a tree, and whipped him until the skin on his back hung in ribbons. Mangas Coloradas, in true Apache fashion, neither flinched nor cried out during the torture. When released, Mangas Coloradas made it back to his group and held a raid ceremony. That night, only a few of the miners escaped with their lives. Soon after, hardly any *Pinda Lick-o-yi* could be found on Apache lands. Mangas Coloradas devoted the rest of his life to avenging the injustice done to him.

Both Cochise and Victorio suffered similar injustices and cruelties at the hands of the Mexicans or the Americans. Unfortunately for the Apaches, all routes to southern California passed through their lands. In addition, that land was soon found to be rich in many valuable metals. It was only a matter of time before the Apache would be pushed onto reservations. Once confined to the reservation, his entire way of life would be changed.

Texas also experienced Indian problems. In Texas the problem was handled very much as it had been in Arizona and New Mexico. First, a series of forts was built. Later, as some of the tribes were defeated, they were placed on reservations. Texas also created the Rangers, a special police force trained to fight the Indians and to guard the thousand-mile Mexican border.

In California, the generally peaceful Indians faced the trials of protecting themselves against the white invaders. The miners had little regard for land ownership. To these men the Treaty of Guadalupe Hidalgo had no real meaning. As the miners overran the Indian lands, the Indians moved to defend their homes and possessions. The Indians, robbed of food-gathering areas, turned into raiders, attacking mining camps to steal food and supplies. The miners in turn banded together to punish the Indians. Finally, the government stepped in and drew up treaties which placed the Indians on reservations.

What took place on the California reservations was typical of reservation life. Most agents in charge knew and cared little about Indian ways, and abused the Indians in their care. Living conditions were dreadful. Thousands of Indians died from disease or lack of food. In endless ways the government failed to uphold its side of the bargain. To this day conditions on the reservations reflect the attitudes that began with the white man's invasion of the Southwest.

Land Grant Claims

In settling the land claims of former Mexican citizens in newly acquired American territory, American authorities ignored Mexican law and customs in favor of familiar methods. In Texas, most of the land grant problems had been worked out during the ten years of the Lone Star Republic. But in California, Arizona, and New Mexico, hundreds of grants remained, both large and small, old and new. For some of the grants there were records; but for most there were not. Precise legal documents were of little use to the Mexican; he knew which were his lands and which were not. Besides, cattle and sheep had been the most important industries, so clear boundaries such as fences were not necessary. Understandably, the new industry—mining—simply could not operate that way.

According to the Treaty of Guadalupe Hidalgo, the United States was required to recognize Mexican land grant titles. The various military governors from Washington, D. C., repeated the promises. Yes, the United States would carry through the terms of the treaty. Yet when this guarantee was put to the test, the commission set up in California in 1852 demanded strict proof of ownership of the *Californios*. As a result, many *Californios* were tied up in court for years, and paid fortunes in legal fees. Many ended up losing most of their lands, some when the judgment went against them, others when they were forced to sell land to pay their lawyers.

The land grant commission assigned three agents to decide on each claim. They knew nothing about cattle raising, the basis of the *Californios'* economy, nor were they clear about how the boundaries for grants were determined. They disputed the reality that the *Californios'* interest in land was for grazing. They jumped to the conclusion that land produced agriculture. Furthermore, the agents were thinking ahead: If the grants were approved as presented by these new Americans, there would be no land for settlers from the East.

The gold rush added a further complication. The miners loudly contributed their feelings of greed and prejudice. If the "greasers" had lost the war, why should they be entitled to hold on to their lands? After all, "To the victor belong the spoils." So tough-minded and determined were these miners that they often resorted to murders and lynchings.

To make matters worse for landowners, squatters often moved onto disputed lands during the legal arguments. It was next to impossible to move them off. The government would help only if the landowner paid the squatters for any improvements made on the land.

The whole business of land grant claims invited fraud. One of the more interesting attempts was made by a Frenchman, José Limantour. Limantour upset the residents of San Francisco by claiming a four league grant (about 16 miles) running through the city center. Limantour presented all the necessary papers and witnesses. If the commission found the claim in order, San Francisco would have had to hand over thousands of dollars to buy itself back. It took two years to uncover the fraud, at which time Limantour left California in a hurry.

The biggest disputes occurred closest to the cities, such as San Francisco and Los Angeles, where property had developed great value. As a result, people fought hard for rights to keep such lands. To further complicate matters, towns and cities had grown so rapidly that records were not able to keep pace.

Within the towns, other controversies arose, most of them based on the question of whether the land belonged to the town itself or to the people within the town. The grants had originally included four leagues surrounding the town. These outlying lands were the biggest issue. Many had been sold by representatives of the American government before the commission arrived. Yet according to the grants, the lands belonged to the pueblo as a whole, and therefore the sales were illegal. To add to the mess, some of this property had been subdivided and resold.

Commission decisions almost always favored the towns. It is easy to see how such rulings caused suffering and bitterness, hurting squatter and landowner alike.

In the end, it was the land lawyers who won. This showed most clearly in New Mexico, where land grant holders were cheated out of millions of acres of land. An infamous group of lawyers known as the "Santa Fe Ring" was within a few years able to grab up 80% of the existing Spanish and Mexican grants. One member of the group helped himself to seventy-five land grants totalling 2,000,000 acres and shared with another lawyer an additional 4,000,000 acres. Probably with the aid of the governor and the surveyor-general, the "Ring" seized the Maxwell Land Grant, a single property covering entire mountains and whole villages within its 1,714,764 acres.

To gain control of the lands, the lawyers simply took full advantage of the people, who did not think of land in terms of money. To them, it was *tierra*. *Tierra,* a Spanish word, translates into English as earth, land, nation, country, dirt, soil, home. The *tierra* was part of them. Their families had lived on it for generations. It belonged to no single man, but to his family for generations past and generations yet to come. Life itself was a beautiful and sensible arrangement between man and nature.

In New Mexico, time became a factor that added to the confusion and provided opportunities for dishonest dealings. Here, land claims were investigated not by a three-man commission but by a surveyor-general, whose job it was to determine the exact size and location of a property. This done, he would submit his findings to Congress for a decision. The surveyor-general worked very slowly. In two years he collected 1,104 claims, but three years later he had surveyed only twenty-five of them.

Nor was the government quick to act on Pueblo Indian claims. By 1858 it had settled seventeen, but it took thirty years to approve an additional 141 Indian claims. The delay meant that millions of acres of land remained in question and untouched. The United States had clearly taken too long to carry out the terms of the Treaty of Guadalupe Hidalgo. Not until 1910 were all the claims decided upon. Finally, of the 30,000,000 acres claimed, only 10,000,000 were accepted. It had taken over half a century to arrange what was to have been determined almost immediately. To this day many claims have not been settled to the satisfaction of those involved. As this book is written a conflict takes place involving claims in Tierra Amarilla in Rio Arriba County of New Mexico.

The Gringo and the Greaser

Much like the early colonizers from Mexico in the 17th and 18th centuries, Anglo American settlers new to the Southwest learned from the inhabitants how to get the most out of the land. The settlers from the East took from the Mexicans' 250 years of experience in making their adjustment to the new lands. In the process of borrowing and adjusting to the Southwest, they changed their way of life. Today the difference between Easterners and Westerners is easily noticed.

Once the rush for gold was over the immigrants began to work towards a secure life. Taking over many of the industries developed by the Mexican settlers, they raised cattle, sheep, horses, and mules. They went into mining, citrus fruit and grape growing, and farming. To make the land produce they had to learn first how to irrigate. Irrigated farming (supplying the land with water by means of ditches or channels) was something new to the settlers from the East. There, rain was plentiful. On the other hand, the Southwest had always suffered from a lack of water. In fact, water was so precious that a system of laws had grown up around water rights. Many of the laws had originated in Spain, where water always had been a matter of great concern.

The oldest irrigation systems still in use in the United States are to be found in the Rio Grande Valley in New Mexico. The earliest settlers were irrigating the land around Las Cruces even before the Pilgrims landed in 1620. The Pueblos and other Indians of the Southwest had used irrigation ditches before the arrival of the Spaniards. Spanish innovations had contributed to the improvements of aqueducts and cisterns and added the building of canals. As the agricultural industry grew, so did further refinements of the irrigation system to support it.

Irrigation requires a great deal of know-how. To prevent wasting water, the soil has to be carefully prepared. Also a farmer must know when and how long to irrigate. The Mexican was a master at the science. The manner of irrigation most commonly used in the Southwest is called the "Mexican system." The process

consists of first leveling the land, then blocking it out in squares; the sides of each square are built up to hold the water. After one block is soaked, a hole is made in the side wall so that the water flows through to soak the next block. The process is repeated until all the blocks are soaked.

Along with irrigation came knowledge about wells, water wheels, *zanjas* (ditches), *acequias* (channels), and the *acequia-madre* (main stream). Anglo Americans adopted most of the existing systems being used for land division, homesteading, and water rights.

The half-century that followed the gold rush to California saw great changes throughout the Southwest as the Anglo American imposed his culture on the Southwest. The imposition seemed a natural order of things to him, since he formed a majority. But to the Mexican American, as he is now called, the changes brought about major shifts in government, defense, land management, school systems, business, law, taxation, and language. To many Mexican Americans, this changing way of life was upsetting and difficult to understand.

The language difference alone created an enormous problem for them. In California the first state constitution was written in both English and Spanish. New settlers found it necessary to learn Spanish in order to get along in the Southwest. As the Anglo American population increased, however, the English language began to take over. So did many of the attitudes suggested by the concept of "manifest destiny." The Anglo American generally believed that his ways were best and expected the people of the Southwest to accept them.

By the late 1850's, the Anglo Americans outnumbered the Mexican Americans by about six to one. The chance for a new Southwest culture—a blend of Indian, Spanish, Mexican, and Anglo American—was weakened by this uneven ratio, which reinforced the lack of understanding and mutual acceptance. The cultures did not blend. As always, misunderstandings led to antagonism, and from antagonism erupted violence. Some instances were large; others were minor. One notable conflict involved the

Blacks of southern Texas. Many of them had fled as slaves into Mexico and had developed a large colony in Matamoros by 1856. From there they hatched a plot to free all the slaves in Texas. Because the Texans believed that the Blacks were being aided by Mexicans, they ordered all Mexicans to leave the counties closest to the Mexican border. In other areas, they prohibited Mexicans from traveling without passes. Before long, Texans were giving voice to the feeling that Mexicans were out to destroy slavery in Texas. As a result most Texans refused to hire any Mexican help and began to complain that "greasers" should never have been given citizenship in the first place. The plot fell apart, but the ill feelings remained.

This incident was followed by another, known as the Cart War. For more than a century, Spaniards and Mexicans had been transporting goods from the Gulf of Mexico to San Antonio and from there to Chihuahua. Their route was known as the Chihuahua Trail, which covered a distance of 1,200 miles, and was reported to be "dustier, drier, hotter, rockier, thornier" than the Santa Fe Trail. By the end of the haul most wagons were completely worn out. Yet, at its peak, the Chihuahua Trail was used by about 200 different companies to transport goods between Chihuahua and the gulf ports. Heading inland the wagons hauled mainly manufactured goods from American and European industries. On the way out they transported gold, silver, copper and lead from the mines of Chihuahua. It was a hard way to make a living, but the total value of one year's cargo of goods and merchandise netted several million dollars for the merchants.

Certain Texans watched this steady and profitable caravan with growing annoyance and envy. The "greasers," after all, made their money by crossing through American territory. The Texans made every attempt to drive them out of business. Bands of them attacked the wagon trains, killing the drivers and stealing the merchandise, and forcing some companies to give up. Complaints from the Mexican government finally succeeded in forcing the United States to send soldiers to protect the wagons on the Chihuahua Trail.

These incidents, and more, added to the antagonism between the "Mexican" and American citizens of Texas. The new Americans began to resent their status. They were, it seemed, Americans in name only. One man, Juan Nepomuceno Cortina, fought a one-man war against Texas. Cortina was a member of a rich and well-known Mexican family living in Texas. Cortina's war began when a Texas sheriff attempted to arrest one of his servants. Juan Cortina would not allow the arrest, and in the fight that followed, he killed the sheriff and freed the servant. The outcome was a ten-year war. Battling against what he called *gringo* injustice, he fought to free

Mexicans imprisoned by the Americans. Mounted on a beautiful horse, Cortina would lead his men as far as 150 miles inland from the Mexican border in a daring raid on a *gringo* jail.

After many luckless attempts over the years to capture Cortina, frustrated and angry Texans began to burn Mexican homes. They justified their actions by accusing the Mexicans of aiding the raider and his men. This charge put pressure on the Mexican government to assist in the hunt for the dashing bandit, but Mexican soldiers were no more fortunate than the Texas Rangers. Finally, the president of Mexico brought the Cortina War to an end in 1873 by making Cortina his personal prisoner. But the ill-feeling and bitterness between *gringo* and "greaser" lived on and deepened.

Other bandit heroes also became famous for their exploits. In California, the name Joaquin Murieta created fear in the hearts of the Anglo Americans. Whether such a man existed is open to question. To the Mexicans, however, he was a hero, a Robin Hood figure, robbing the rich and giving to the poor. Stories about Murieta grew so colorful and terrifying as to be ridiculous. For example, on occasions he was positively identified as being in three places at the same time. Prospectors and gold miners lived in mortal fear of his riding in on them at any moment. One Anglo American, apparently afraid that any Mexican he saw might be a bandit, put it this way:

> "When I see a Mexican approaching, I cock my rifle and cover him with it, and at the same time calling to him to raise his hand away from his lasso, which hangs at his saddle-bow. In this way, I keep my rifle on him until he has gone beyond lasso distance."

Among others who fought against "*gringo* injustice" were Luis Bulvia, Antonio Moreno, Procopio Soto, Manuel Garcia, Juan Flores, Tiburcio Vasquez. Vasquez, before being executed in 1852, explained his actions in this frank manner:

"A spirit of hatred and revenge took possession of me. I had numerous fights in defense of what I believed to be my rights and those of my countrymen. I believed we were being unjustly deprived of the social rights that belonged to us."

As could well be expected, the Anglo Americans fought back. In 1857, in Los Angeles, eleven Mexicans were lynched; in El Monte another four. The practice of lynching Mexicans became so commonplace, in fact, that newspapers often did not consider the news important enough to print. Many of these bandit-heroes live on in *corridos* (ballads). A *corrido* generally tells a story about a man involved in a conflict against great odds. *Corridos* have always been popular among Mexicans. Today they deal with the modern Mexican American. The following is a good example of a *corrido*, this one dating back many years.

El Corrido de Gregorio Cortez

In the county of El Carmen
A great misfortune befell;
The Major Sheriff is dead;
Who killed him no one can tell.

At two in the afternoon,
In half an hour or less,
They knew that the man who killed him
Had been Gregorio Cortez.

They let loose the bloodhound dogs;
They followed him from afar.
But trying to catch Cortez
Was like following a star.

All the rangers of the county
Were flying, they rode so hard;
What they wanted was to get
The thousand dollar reward.

And in the county of Kiansis
They cornered him after all;
Though they were more than three hundred
He leaped out of their corral.

Then the Major Sheriff said,
As if he was going to cry,
"Cortez, hand over your weapons;
We want to take you alive."

Then said Gregorio Cortez,
And his voice was like a bell,
"You will never get my weapons
Till you put me in a cell."

Then said Gregorio Cortez,
With his pistol in his hand,
"Ah, so many mounted Rangers
Just to take one Mexican!"

This chapter has attempted to illustrate the sharp contrasts between Aztlán/The Southwest and the United States. The United States, in winning the war against Mexico, gained the lands of the Southwest but not an understanding of its peoples. Close contact between the cultures only brought more sharply into focus the differences between them. Because of the war, the Americans were able to enter as conquerors disregarding the way of life they found, and ignoring laws and property rights. Indeed, most Americans regarded Aztlán simply as the "spoils of war" and consistently violated the Treaty of Guadalupe Hidalgo.

The Americans had no awareness that the signing of the treaty had created a new people. The new people were Spanish-speaking American citizens with a culture different from that of the English-speaking Americans. This lack of awareness made them see the Spanish-speaking Americans as a conquered people, and therefore an "inferior" people.

In consequence, one must ask this necessary question: What effect did the Anglo American attitude have on the Spanish-speaking American? This question raises another important one: What was the effect on the Indian when both Spanish and English-speaking Americans regarded him as "savage"?

7

The Mexican American

El Barrio

I'm that piece of land *la ciudad** is trying to hide;
I house *gente* to whom the American dream has lied,
in my corners stand the youth *morena* with no future,
in *callejón* walls graffiti find their nomenclature.
My aroma of hunger brings *muerte* to the table,
Monday's wash on the *tendedores* tells a torn fable
as a *chisme* dripping away from old women's parched mouths.
I act as a stereo amplifying clearly *dolor* shouts.
My *calles* shudder littered with the weight of many needs.
My *ambiente* is a constant S O S no one heeds. . . .

Abelardo

* Glossary: *la ciudad* = the city, *gente* = people, *morena* = dark, brunette,
callejón = alley, *muerte* = death, *tendedores* = clotheslines,
chisme = gossip, *dolor* = pain, sorrow, *calles* = streets, *ambiente*
= environment

PART I—TO BECOME A MINORITY

The Barrio

The development of the Southwest moved along under the leadership of the incoming Anglo Americans. The Mexican Americans found they had become a minority and withdrew into communities called *colonias* or *barrios* (colonies and neighborhoods). There, they shut themselves away from the Anglo Americans, leading a separate way of life. The *barrio* was generally the oldest part of the town or city. Outsiders often referred to it by disrespectful names, such as Spiktown, Greaser Heaven, or simply, the other side of the tracks. The Mexican American used other terms: Sonora Town (in memory of the Mexican state), *Sal-si-puedes* (Get-out-if-you-can), or El Hoyo (The Hole).

The Mexican Americans did not choose isolation; it was forced on them. A growing pattern of events had made this clear. They suffered injustices from sheriffs, Rangers, and ordinary citizens. They were often to find labor conditions harder for them than for any other group. They were to face times of ignorance, prejudice, and hatred impossible to withstand. Mexican Americans were offered no way to become part of the Anglo American community.

The Salt War of 1877, at El Paso on the Rio Grande, offers a good example of conflict between the two groups. At this time, El Paso was completely Mexican, except for 80 people, a fact that bothered many Anglos. About 100 miles east of the town was the salt mine, discovered by a Mexican in 1862. Its Mexican owners had always been generous to El Paso, allowing residents free salt for their personal needs. This custom was to change suddenly.

With the end of the war in 1850, a few Anglo Americans moved in and took over the government. Soon they began acquiring nearly everything else. One Anglo American somehow gained hold of the mine and quickly demanded that the people of El Paso pay for their "personal" salt. Furious at being deprived of this important gift, the people rose up to seize the city. Their leader was a priest, Father Borajo. In the fight that followed, three *gringos* were killed, and thousands of dollars worth of property was destroyed. In the return fight, the Anglo Americans killed as many "greasers" and lynched several before order was finally restored. The bitterness and hatred continued.

There were many other incidents, all of them adding to the basic tension between Mexican American and Anglo American. The Texas Rangers, proud of their policy of avenging an attack on one of their number ten times over, were really creating ten times the grounds for more attacks. From about 1866 to 1880, a continuous "war" raged between Mexicans and Anglo Americans. Much of the fighting was over cattle and land, with each side raiding the other's herds. The Mexicans made a habit of retreating across the border to the Mexican side. On more than one occasion, American soldiers were sent in pursuit. When Mexican herds were rustled, the "beef packeries" on the American side would purchase the cattle and ignore the brands on the hides. Therefore, the Mexicans had little regard for political boundaries. (Even today, many Mexicans and Mexican Americans see the Southwest or Aztlán as being one land.) To raid Texas was easy for them. The Texans, who did not have the same feelings, were generally afraid to cross the border.

Mexican Americans, not reluctant to poke fun at their adversaries, put together a number of *corridos* that took note of the clashes between themselves and the *gringos*. Any Mexican American who came out on top in such a skirmish, especially if Rangers were involved, soon found himself the hero of a *corrido*. Here is one such *corrido*:

Corrido de Jacinto Treviño
(*Translated by Americo Paredes*)

It happened once in McAllen
In San Benito, that's twice,
Now it has happened in Brownsville,
And we have seen something nice.

In that saloon known as Baker's
The bullets started to fly;
Bottles would jump into pieces
Wherever you set your eye.

In that saloon known as Baker's
They scatter and they run;
No one is left but Jacinto
With rifle and pistol-gun.

"Come on, you cowardly Rangers;
No baby is up agin' you.
You wanted to meet your daddy?
I am Jacinto Treviño!

"Come on, you treacherous Rangers;
Come get a taste of my lead.
And did you think it was ham
Between two slices of bread?"[1]

The sheriff was an American,
But he was shouting aloud,
"You are a brave man, Jacinto;
You make the Mexicans proud."

Then said Jacinto Treviño,
Laughing so hard that it hurt,
"Why don't you kiss my elbow
And fold the cuffs of my shirt!"

Then said Jacinto Treviño,
Taking a drink from a spring,
"Oh, what a poor bunch of Rangers
They didn't do me a thing!"

Then said Jacinto Treviño,
"Now it is time to retire
I'm going to Rio Grande
And I will welcome you there."

Now I must beg your permission,
This is the end of the chorus;
I am Jacinto Treviño
A native of Matamoros.

In the spring of 1875, one band of Mexicans launched a big raid. In return the Americans attacked Mexican communities, burning homes and shooting innocent people. One writer described the attack: "Large parties of mounted and well-armed men committed the most brutal outrages, murdering peaceful Mexican farmers and stockmen who had lived all their lives in Texas." The American counter-blow was fierce enough to slow down Mexican raids. Raiding, however, continued until 1900.

The period following the American Civil War aggravated conditions for the Mexican. (Few Mexicans participated in the Civil War. Here and there came some volunteers, mostly from wealthy Mexican families. On the whole, the draft had little effect on people in the far west.) The Southwest offered a new chance for the defeated southerners. Unfortunately, they brought with

---

[1] Ham . . . bread: Mexicans think American ham sandwiches are a joke.

them not only the bitterness of defeat but also their attitudes about "inferior races." The Indians, especially the Apache, viewed this new group as more of the hated "white eyes." The Mexicans saw the southerners as *gringos* favoring slavery. And slavery, the Mexicans knew, was based on color differences. The southerners made many Mexicans painfully aware of their own dark skins, adding still another cause for tension and misunderstanding.

As more Anglo Americans moved into the Southwest, the natives of Aztlán were reduced as a percentage of the total population. Furthermore, few areas were left to the Mexicans. Along the Texas-New Mexico border, wars often broke out between sheepmen and cattlemen. The majority of the sheepmen were Mexicans. During these running battles, both Mexicans and Anglo Americans were killed. The Mexican was generally the first to withdraw for he had no support. Eventually, even sheepherding was closed to the Mexican.

In Arizona, mine development drew flocks of Anglos. Soon the Mexican was given only the lowliest jobs at the mines. The value of the Mexican as a working man sank further with the completion of the railroads. The Santa Fe and Southern Pacific railroads, cutting through the heart of the Southwest, had depended heavily on Mexican labor. But their very skill and hard work brought a successful end to railroad construction, leaving thousands of Spanish-speaking workers unemployed.

Most Anglo Americans resented these jobless people, looking down on them as a burden to the community. Often the hostile feelings between *gringos* and "greasers" would reach the boiling point, and might well end with a lynching to keep the Mexicans "in their place." It was in the *barrio* that the Mexican American did find his "place."

There, Mexican Americans established their own way of life, a way different from both the Mexican and Anglo American cultures. It was unique. Yet the surrounding lifestyles could not help but influence *barrio* life. The material side of Anglo American ways, the "hard culture," gradually took hold. Objects and possessions that were distinctly Mexican in origin were slowly replaced. The effects were seen in home furniture, clothing, food, and other everyday necessities. The "soft culture," the deep-down attitudes towards family, social relations, spiritual beliefs and practices, basically stayed closer to traditional Mexican ways.

The binding factor of the Spanish language press always provided lively news of the community, constant reminders of their separateness, and frequent promptings to react boldly against the *gringo*.

Life in the *barrio* always appears strange to the outsider traveling through it. To a Mexican American, life there is comfortable and familiar. Outside the *barrio,* many Spanish-speaking people feel strangers in their own land.

The growth of the *barrios* did not displease the Anglo Americans, for it made the Mexican American easier to ignore. When society ignores a person, or a people, it fails to provide for his needs. So it was with both the Mexican American and the Indian.

The American Indians were openly isolated by being placed on reservations and virtually forgotten. With the Mexican Americans, it was different; they were simply pushed into the background little by little.

Like most minorities in America, Mexican Americans had to be identified in order to be overlooked. Their visibility, the so-called "Mexican look," was often distinctive. In other cases, their language marked them. For still others, it was their surname. These three characteristics helped to single out the Mexican Americans as a group. As time went by, the group was forgotten more and more in terms of their rights in the community. When they were finally remembered, it was not for the sake of justice, it was as a source of cheap labor.

Migrant Labor

With the growth of industry in the east, labor became a vital need. Prospering industrial centers offered broad opportunities for needy European immigrants and migrant labor flocked to the cities. One natural result of the population growth was an increase in the need for food and raw materials in the east.

Many of these essentials could be most easily supplied by the Southwest. In fact, the Southwest seemed a perfect place for agriculture. One crop, cotton, was especially desirable. The demand for cotton by the eastern mills replaced the former need for cattle. By 1900, the great cattle boom had died down; the market was over-supplied. The vast lands no longer supported huge herds of cattle. Now they were given over to cotton.

Cotton had been grown in east Texas from the time of the Southerners' settlement there in the early 1800's. Now the industry spread to middle and west Texas. But the operation of the fields differed with the growers. In east Texas, cotton growers employed Black labor and ran their operations plantation style. Cotton growers of middle and west Texas areas required other methods of cultivation and irrigation. These growers began to rely on migrant Mexican labor.

Migrant farm labor consisted of workers who moved from one farm to another following the demand for labor. Because they were only temporary help, they could ask little of the farmer for upkeep. They seldom had real houses to live in, only shacks or tents. The cheapness of Mexican migrant labor plus the growth of the cotton industry caused this segment of the population to increase rapidly.

Developments in the cotton industry were only partly responsible for the sudden interest in Mexican labor. Another expanding enterprise was large-scale food farming. The need for fresh fruit, grains and vegetables created a boom in the open lands of the Southwest. The big problem was how to deliver fresh produce to markets thousands of miles away. The answer, of course, was to extend and improve the railroads.

Mexicans provided the labor force for the expansion of the Southern Pacific and Santa Fe lines. Again, thousands of people were brought in from Mexico, many of them to spend their entire lives bouncing around in boxcars. As the railroads reached into various parts of the Southwest, the railroad migrants moved, too, eventually following the lines into Colorado, Wyoming, Utah, Montana, Idaho, Oregon and Washington. Shortly after, railroad lines reaching the west fitted their cars with the new invention, refrigeration. Produce now remained fresh even after traveling for weeks.

The Southwest proved an ideal location for large-scale farming. Space was apparently endless. The climate allowed a year-round growing season. The beautiful valleys had an abundant supply of water. Valleys like the San Joaquin in California, the Mesilla in New Mexico and the San Luis in Colorado became agricultural centers. The government construction of giant reservoirs turned once-arid lands into giant gardens. Thus, the agricultural centers of the Southwest served the industrial centers of the east.

The building of reservoirs, the construction of railroad lines, the cultivation of essential crops—all depended upon available Mexican labor, much of it migratory. Mexican migrants were not organized. They belonged to no particular town, community or company. As a result, they were not well provided for. Most Mexican migrants had no voice about their wages. They and their children had no suitable schooling. They had no say about the system that governed them. Migrants were looked upon simply as labor, despite the fact that many were born in the United States or were married to American citizens.

For the crops raised in the Southwest, the cheapest form of hand labor was essential. An acre of lettuce, for example, required more than 25 man-hours of cultivating to harvest; an acre of strawberries, 500 man-hours. To keep down the price of these items, hourly wages had to be small.

Grape cultivation requires an incredible amount of hand labor and care. Grapes are started with cuttings, whether raised for juice, wine, raisins or table fruit. The small shoots are planted by hand, each at a measured distance from the others. As the cuttings sprout into vines, the workers set up stakes to support the heavy stems or "arms." To train young vines into the right shape, they prune the arms and tie them to the supports. Once a year, men repeat the pruning, taking off almost 9 percent of the past year's growth. They usually leave the spurs or the cane to adjust the quality and quantity of the crops.

Men carry out steady rounds of thinning the budding clusters of grapes in order to increase the size and coloring. Another hand process is the girdling, or ringing, of the vine trunk or arms. This too, increases the yield of the vine. Because of little rain, workers must constantly weed around the vines, so that the grapes will get their full measure of the vital moisture. Then comes the battle against insects, or mildew and other diseases. When ripe, the grapes are readied for the particular purpose for which they were grown. Table grapes are harvested in the hottest part of the summer. Grape pickers handle the clusters gently, trimming them to a certain size and putting them in orderly rows in wooden boxes. To make raisins, the grapes are picked, placed on wooden or paper trays and allowed to dry in the sun. The slow process involves turning the grapes until all are three-quarters dry. California has become the top producer in the United States of grapes in all their forms, due mainly to the work of hand laborers.

Mexican Americans provided the needed hand labor for the prospering agricultural industry. They were readily available in the various communities of the Southwest where their inferior status had prepared them to be usable for this function. Had Mexican Americans shared the full benefits of citizenship, the industry would have had to look elsewhere for cheap labor. In fact, when the industry needed more help than Mexican Americans could provide, the United States government stepped in, relaxing its strict immigration laws to permit the importation of cheap labor from the Orient. But Mexican Americans remained the greatest source of migrant labor.

The railroad industry continued its expansion. Tracks were laid through the fertile lands, providing growers with easy transportation for their produce. Mexican American laborers cleared the land; they laid the ties and tracks; they walked the lines. When the trains made their stops, laborers repaired and maintained the freight cars. Maintenance centers established at these stops became permanent communities. The place names along the routes of the Santa Fe railroad, the Southern Pacific and others still mark towns started by Mexican American laborers. Wherever a labor camp grew, a "Mexican" *colonia* exists today.

In the forty-five years between 1880 and 1925, many agricultural industries developed in the Southwest. Most of them grew and prospered as a direct result of Mexican American labor. The cotton industry spread from Texas to New Mexico and California. The beet industry came into being in California and Colorado. Citrus fruit became a multi-million dollar business. Numerous other crops contributed to the area's agricultural prosperity. The conversion of the Southwest from a desert land into a highly productive industrial nursery had been accomplished by the hand labor of Mexican American workers.

Conditions were almost always bad for the laborers. After working long, hot hours in the fields, the typical migrant worker and his family lived in "camps." These camps offered bad housing, no recreation, no stores, no medical help, no sanitation. The workers' overseer, or foreman, was paid on the basis of how much they produced. The farmers rarely concerned themselves about their temporary help. To them, the people were labor, not human beings. This same attitude was held in surrounding communities, where the migrant workers were not welcome.

The workers had no one to turn to for help, support, interest, or kindness. Their only contact was the labor merchant, who made his living from selling their labor to farmers, and farmers counted their profits in terms of how little money they paid to get the job done. No wonder, then, that the labor merchant was called the *coyote*. His profit lay in the difference between the farmer's contract price and what he actually paid the laborers.

In 1910 Mexico found itself in the grip of a terrible revolution that had grown out of a people's struggle to free themselves from oppression. The revolution virtually destroyed the country, as one man after another took control, each claming that he could provide Mexico with the right leadership. Each leader had an army to back up his claim. Few areas escaped this bloody and destructive civil war. The fighting even went on along the United States-Mexican border, sometimes spilling over into the United States. These incidents added to the bad feelings between "greasers" and *gringos*.

The Revolution lasted from 1910 to 1922. Thousands fled Mexico. The first five years saw nearly 72,000 Mexicans enter the United States to escape the destruction and violence. They became part of the answer to the labor shortage in the United States created by World War I (1914–18), which drained America's labor pool and created an enormous demand for workers.

Industrial areas in all parts of the United States began to take advantage of the flood of cheap labor. Chicago brought in thousands of Mexican Americans and Mexican immigrants to work in the meat packing plants, tanneries and steel mills. Detroit transported masses for the automobile industry. Ohio and Pennsylvania hired them for the steel mills. The copper mines of Arizona employed thousands more. Railroads throughout the nation used great numbers to maintain their lines.

Some of these refugees went in family groups. Generally the women worked as domestics in Anglo American households. They also worked in clothing factories or other light industries. Both men and women earned unbelievably low pay even for those times. Hard working fieldhands received as little as twelve and one-half cents an hour, although sometimes the rate went up to thirty cents. A team of cotton pickers got $5.00 a bale for their heavy task. Refugees from the Revolution would work for any salary they could get. Despite the growing tide of refugees there was still a labor shortage. The government, therefore, began to import more and more cheap labor from Mexico into the Southwest.

These sudden waves of cheap labor created a new issue. Some Mexican Americans had managed to gain higher wages, and thus improve their living conditions. Now, with all the cheap labor around, they were looked at as being just more "Mexicans," and were forced to accept the low wages paid to the immigrants.

In light of the enormous burden of labor these people carried, it is difficult to understand the reasons for the stereotype of the "lazy Mexican." This distorted image has served time and again for putting down Mexicans and Mexican Americans. It has been used to characterize them in movies, television, and comic strips. It has been reproduced in trademarks. It has served as the butt of countless jokes.

At first, most of those who came as laborers or refugees expected to go home to Mexico after things had returned to normal in their own country. The Revolution lasted so long that many of them settled permanently, making their homes and raising their American-born children in the *barrios*. The *barrios* grew larger, especially in the big cities. Today the *barrios* of San Antonio, Las Cruces, and Tucson have populations of several thousands. The Los Angeles *barrio* has a population of over half a million.

The migration of Mexicans came to a halt during the Great Depression. The Depression, which lasted from 1930 through 1938, threw millions of Americans out of work. In an attempt to ease the pressures of unemployment, the government adopted a cheap and seemingly simple solution. Thousands of Mexican laborers were deported to Mexico. Many were forced to take their families with them, even though most of their children had been born in the United States. Among the deported laborers were many United States citizens. If a person looked "Mexican," the authorities had reason enough to deport him.

Deportation was also used as a convenient way to get rid of "troublemakers." During the Depression, farm workers held strikes to obtain better wages and improved living conditions. The new immigrants had families born in the United States, which meant that their children now had rights equal to any other citizen. Why should their children be set apart, regarded as cheap labor, or inferiors, as their parents were? Many Mexican Americans began to organize in order to protect themselves and their children's future. As their weapon of protest they used the strike.

Attempts to seek such a change had come in 1903 when over a thousand Mexican and Japanese sugar beet workers struck in Ventura, California, in a move for better wages and working conditions. In 1910, the Mexican railroad workers went on strike in Los Angeles. The grape-pickers in Fresno attempted to organize a union in 1922. None of these early attempts to seek change or improvement was very successful.

Not until 1927 was a formal organization put together. Its name was the *Confederación de Uniones Obreras Mexicanas* (Confederation of Mexican Workers Unions). The CUOM, as it was known, was formed by 3,000 workers. The first strike called by the new union was in Imperial Valley, California, in 1929. The farmers fought back by having Mexican workers deported. Two years later the CUOM again went on strike in Imperial Valley against the melon growers. This time they took the farmers by surprise. The farm workers made these demands:

1. 15¢ per standard crate of melons or 75¢ an hour.
2. Growers to supply free picking racks and ice.
3. Growers to pay for workmen's compensation.
4. Wages earned by the workers to be deposited in a bank and not given to the labor merchant.

This last demand was very important. The job of labor merchant or contractor was to supply the farmers with a work crew. These *coyotes* too often were crooks and would frequently disappear with all the money. The farmers never asked any questions. This strike forced the farmers to make some changes.

In 1933, seven thousand Mexican American workers went on strike against the berry, onion and celery growers near Los Angeles. It was the largest strike ever called by any group of farm workers. Many people were amazed that the Mexican American would stand up and fight for a fair deal. This strike caused a chain reaction among workers in the rich San Joaquin Valley of California, who fought against "race discrimination, poor working conditions and low pay."

Many of these strikes resulted in violence. On more than one occasion tear gas was used to break up meetings. In addition to mass arrests and deportations, a number of killings took place.

Strikes were not limited to the agricultural industry. In Arizona the copper mining industry was struck as early as 1896. As with the farm workers, the fight was against discrimination, poor pay and bad working conditions.

Discrimination took many forms. Some companies specified two types of workers, *white* and *Mexican*. For performing the same task, white workers received a higher salary than the Mexicans. Some companies would not hire Mexicans until all available whites had jobs. This method was known as last-one-hired-first-one-fired. Often Mexicans were not allowed to live in the community in which they worked although local merchants were eager to take their money. Still another form of discrimination involved opening only certain unpleasant or unskilled jobs to Mexicans.

Rarely was any effort made to provide real safety measures for the Mexican American worker. Many times there were no water or sanitation facilities. Medical aid was practically unknown. Children were expected to work as hard and long as adults. Housing was a disgrace. The hours were long. Bonus pay for overtime was unheard of. Many Mexicans and Mexican Americans have served as leaders in the fight against such inhuman working conditions. Among such men was Jesús Pallares, a Mexican.

Jesús Pallares

At fifteen Jesús had left his home to fight in the Revolution on the side of those striving for human rights. In 1915, a wound had cost him part of his lower jaw and forced him out of the fight. He entered the United States legally to become a part of the labor force imported during World War I. Jesús went to work as a miner. His record indicates that he was an excellent worker, much liked by his supervisors. Only during the Depression was he ever without a job. Jesús had definite beliefs about the need to correct bad working conditions. The only way to achieve change for the better, he felt, was through an organization such as a recognized union which would have the power to bargain and make contracts.

Jesús' first real attempt at unionizing workers occurred in Madrid, New Mexico, where he had found work during the early days of the Depression. Madrid was a company town. The miners' homes were old shacks with rotten floors, leaking roofs, and no indoor plumbing. For this, the miners paid the company $60 per room per year. Miners could live only in company houses. Most miners were paid in scrip rather than cash. This scrip was a form of private money that could be spent only in the company store. The explosives used by the miners to break loose the coal had to be paid for in the scrip they earned. Miners earned only eighty cents a ton for the coal they dug and were forced to pay $3.00 a month for coal to use in their homes. Because of endless other company charges, many miners became indebted to the company. This was precisely what the owners wanted, for it gave them complete control of the workers. The workers were not allowed to leave until their debts had been settled.

In 1933, the conditions at Madrid became so bad that the miners went on strike. Jesús helped sneak in organizers and soon acquired organizing skills of his own. In turn, the company soon learned of his role in the strike and began to make trouble for him. The strike went on with Jesús leading it. In spite of great efforts, the company refused to give in and recognize the union. Eventually, the miners had to give up their strike. Although Jesús could not legally be fired for his union organizing activities, the company got their revenge by making him dig in places that produced poor yields of coal. His wife was expecting their fifth child and his earnings were so low that he could not pay his rent. All his savings had gone for food. The company threw him out and blacklisted him, which meant that he could not get a job as a miner.

Jesús would not give up. He still believed the answer to workers' problems was a strong union. In the fall of 1934 he began the *Liga Obreras de Habla Española* (The Spanish-Speaking Workers League) with 300 workers. By 1935, the union was 8,000 strong, and was powerful enough to bring to a stop the work in all the mines of the area. The mining companies managed to introduce a bill in the New Mexican legislature making certain types of union activity a crime. The law would have been passed, but when the final vote was being taken, members of *Liga* marched into the Capitol. This show of force so upset the politicians that they voted against the bill. Jesús Pallares and the *Liga* tasted their first victory.

However, Jesús was now in deep trouble, for the mining interests and politicians of New Mexico saw him as a threat. Matters became worse for him when he was elected to organize the whole state. The politicians made up a case which charged Jesús with being an undesirable alien and had him arrested on deportation charges in April, 1935. However, the case fell apart and the charges were dropped. Still Jesús continued his work with the *Liga*, despite harassment to him and his family.

Jesús was again brought to trial. This time the charge was that the *Liga* seemed to be part of a Communist organization. Another piece of evidence was simply an opinion: when on strike, the *Liga* might cost human lives. On this body of "evidence" Jesús was found guilty of being an undesirable alien and was deported on June 29, 1935.

Jesús Pallares had spent twenty-three of his thirty-nine years as a skilled miner. For nineteen of those years he had worked the mines in and around Gallup, New Mexico. Of the remaining four years, he had spent two in school. The last two years he had been forced to go on welfare. He had married and raised a family of six children, all born in the United States. It is difficult today to see him in a negative light.

The fights for better working conditions have continued for nearly half a century. In many ways the Mexican American has contributed most to the improved working conditions for all field laborers, farm workers, miners and other skilled workers in the Southwest.

Braceros and Agribusiness

The end of the Depression was followed by America's entrance into World War II in 1941. The war caused manpower shortages everywhere. The agricultural industry called loudly for help, and once again, the United States turned to Mexico. Mexican farm labor entered the country this time as *braceros* (strong-armed or day laborers). The *bracero* program was organized between the United States and Mexico, with each government providing regulations for the operation. People who hired *braceros* had to put up a bond of $50.00 for each worker. Another rule ordered the farmer or contractor to pay a set wage. *Braceros* were not limited to farm work. Some railroad companies also contracted for them.

By 1944, when the war was at its peak, the United States had contracted for nearly 63,000 *braceros,* most of them from the poorer sections of Mexico. The Mexican government planned that their earnings would improve living conditions there by bringing in new money.

On the surface the program seemed to benefit everyone concerned, but it actually hurt the migrant workers, who now had to compete against this cheaper source of labor. The *braceros,* although paid less, were given more. Their housing and transportation were free. Furthermore, they did not have to continue to live in the United States. As soon as the job was done, they returned to Mexico. Migrants who had homes and families in the United States had a much higher cost of living.

The *bracero* had troubles, too. He was often the victim of dishonest farmers and contractors. To get into the *bracero* program, some workers had to pay bribes. Many times contractors deducted the cost of the bond from a man's wages. As imported labor, *braceros* had no rights. They could not turn to the law for help.

World War II ended, but the *bracero* program did not. The agribusiness, as it was now being called, considered the program necessary for its continued success. The farmers even claimed that the *bracero* was better at stoop labor than the Mexican American. By 1957, nearly half a million *braceros* had entered the United States.

An added hardship for the Mexican American was another new form of cheap labor—the "wetback"—Mexican nationals who

slipped into the United States illegally to seek work. It was easy enough for these Mexicans to wade or swim the Rio Grande, which forms a large part of the border. Hence the name wetbacks. The wetbacks were not a group. They were individuals who could not get jobs as *braceros* because they did not live near the contracting centers or who did not have enough money to pay off the contractors. Many were taken across the border by smugglers. Smuggling wetbacks past the immigration authorities became a big business. To avoid detection, smugglers sometimes locked the illegal aliens in refrigerator trucks or airless vans causing many tragic deaths. Stories of such brutal treatment by smugglers fill police records of the various states along the border.

It is estimated that in 1953 about 886,000 men entered the United States illegally from Mexico. Needless to say, most of them became victims of poor working conditions, bad wages and harsh treatment. All of them lived in fear of the *migra,* their name for the immigration authority. Knowing this, employers in the agribusiness would work the illegal aliens until just before payday, then call the *migra* and turn them in. Meanwhile, Mexican Americans suffered increasingly as the number of wetbacks grew. To those in the agribusiness he was just another wetback or *bracero,* just so much cheap stoop labor.

During the period after World War II, agricultural unions began to develop and grow. Men such as Ernesto Galarza and Cesar Chavez became leaders in the union movement, with Chavez becoming most active in recent times.

Ernesto Galarza is an unusual man. Like many leaders in the Mexican American community, Dr. Galarza came to the United States from Mexico during the Mexican Revolution. His family settled in Sacramento, California. It was a rough road for young Ernesto. Like many young Mexicans in the United States, he had to work his way through school. When his parents died, he had to support his brothers and sisters. Still he did not give up his ambition. It took him longer than most, but after establishing a brilliant academic record, he received his doctoral degree in 1943.

All his life Dr. Galarza has worked hard for the agricultural worker—the Mexican American, the *bracero,* and the wetback alike. In the worst of his many battles for the workers against the agribusiness, he cried out:

"Can't they see? I love this country in a way people don't if they are born here, and take it for granted, and have never seen what things are like anywhere else. I love this country because, for all things wrong, it comes close—close enough to glimpse what the good society might be like. The best way I can possibly imagine to show my respect and affection is to come closer yet—to help get over that remaining gap."

Dr. Galarza fought the *bracero* program because of what it did to all Mexicans and Mexican Americans. His has not been an easy fight. At times the battle has come close to costing him his life. Dr. Galarza has had to fight the agribusiness, the politicians, even the Mexican government, for each of these groups supported the *bracero* movement. To the agribusiness it was a form of cheap labor. To the politicians, it promised the agribusiness vote. To the Mexican government, it meant millions of dollars coming into Mexico. Reports show that in 1963 the *braceros* working for the railroads alone received $63,000,000 in wages.

Dr. Galarza continued his fight. He studied and recorded his findings concerning the dangerous effects of the *bracero* program. He wrote books and articles, and helped to organize the National Agricultural Workers Union. To this day Dr. Galarza remains actively involved in helping the Mexican American worker. The *bracero* program finally came to an end on December 31, 1964, twenty-two years after it started.

The problems faced by the Mexican American workers did not come to an end on December 31, 1964. Another form of Mexican cheap labor still affects them directly. These are the green and blue card carriers, Mexican nationals living in Mexican communities directly across the border from American towns or cities. (Examples of such paired communities are El Paso, Texas and Ciudad Juarez; Douglas, Arizona and Agua Prieta; Laredo, Texas and Nuevo Laredo; Calexico, California and Mexicali.) These workers show their cards to the border guards when they cross into the United States. The card color determines how far away from the border they may work. Blue limits them to a distance of about twenty miles; green allows them as much as 200 miles. The green card carriers are permitted to live in the United States but they must return regularly to Mexico. At the end of a day's work, the blue card carriers must return to Mexico.

This cheap labor source works to the advantage of stateside employers, who do not have to pay sickness or retirement benefits required by law for American citizens. Additionally, these workers usually shop at American stores, leaving behind a good portion of their earnings. On the other hand, this cheap labor hurts American citizens, mainly Mexican Americans, in need of work in these areas. Mexican Americans cannot maintain a decent standard of living on the wages paid to the card carriers. Many Mexican American leaders such as Ernesto Galarza and Cesar Chavez as well as labor unions have attempted to correct this with limited success.

A New Self Image

World War II brought other changes in terms of the Mexican Americans and labor. Aviation, shipbuilding and all forms of construction had moved into full production. Millions of men and women had to be quickly trained to fill defense jobs. Among them were thousands of Mexican Americans who became skilled industrial workers. With the war's end, however, they found themselves once again threatened with the familiar last-one-hired-the-first-one-fired policy.

Some 300,000 to 500,000 Mexican American servicemen fought in all parts of the world. No other single group received so many decorations for valor. Neither did any other group suffer such a high percentage of deaths. Mexican American servicemen gained new views of life, thanks to the war. For some it was their first real venture outside the *barrio;* for most it was their first view of the outside world. In most places they did not feel "different," for there was little discrimination based on their visibility, the way they spoke English or their Spanish names. They were accepted simply as Americans serving their country. The new sense of identity growing out of the war experience determined for many Mexican Americans that, once home, there would be changes. Yet, when they returned they had first to confront the bitterness created by the "zoot suit riots."

The "zoot suit riots" occurred during the early years of World War II and were provoked by Mexican American youth angry over discrimination. These young people of the *barrio* formed gangs and adopted the "zoot suit" as a uniform. The zoot suit was easily recognizable. The pants were full and flared, with tight cuffs; the waist line reached to mid-chest. The long coat had a pinched waist and very wide lapels, with heavily padded shoulders. The suit was generally worn with a dark shirt and a colorful tie.

The zoot suiters developed their own way of life called the *Pachuco.* The origin of the name is not clear, although some say that it came from Pachuca, a city in Mexico. Possibly the name comes from El Paso, where some people of the *barrio* were called *Pachucos,* and where the subculture started. The *Pachucos* developed their own customs and a language made up of English, Spanish, El Paso slang, and the jive talk popular in the late 1930's and early 1940's. Examples are: *refinar*—to eat; *bato, bata*—guy, gal; *jefe, jefa*—father, mother; *garras*—clothes; *chante*—house, home; *guachar*—to look at, to look out.

The *Pachucos,* with their exotic garb and their gang activities, offended nearly everyone, particularly the Anglo American—and especially the serviceman. Times were tense, and those who did not act or dress like "good Americans" were singled out for scorn and hatred. Angry words led to physical attack. One fight led to another, sometimes resulting in injuries and deaths. Often the police looked the other way when the *Pachucos* were getting the worst of it. Clashes between the *Pachucos* and the servicemen grew into riots, while the newspapers blew the riots up beyond their real dimensions. Particularly in Los Angeles and San Diego, the "Zoot Suit Riots" remained a sore issue for a long time.

Returning Mexican American veterans had to overcome hostile attitudes on both sides of the matter. Yet the *Pachucos,* in their bitterness and anger, did focus attention on an American minority that had been forgotten.

These Mexican American veterans were quite different from the men who had left. Their experiences had given them a new feeling about themselves and their future. Many attended college or trade school, taking advantage of the G. I. Bill, a government program that paid for an ex-serviceman's education as well as a good portion of his living expenses while he learned. Another section of the G. I. Bill provided mortgage loans with which Mexican American veterans could purchase homes outside of the *barrio* in newly developing communities.

The new life was not always simple. Many of the returning servicemen or veterans found that they could not qualify for college because of their weak educational background. They also came into contact with people who would not accept them as equals. A mountain of obstacles, mostly relating to discrimination, had yet to be overcome.

It soon became clear to each Mexican American veteran that one man alone could not fight unfair hiring and real estate practices. Organization was needed. Community groups had been meeting as early as the 1920's and 1930's. However, they did not have real strength until the veterans began to join them. One such organization was LULAC (League of United Latin American Citizens).

LULAC was formed in 1929 in Harliner, Texas. Its purpose at the time was to improve the education of Mexican American children. CSO (Community Service Organization) was another. The CSO had started in Los Angeles, originating as a group effort to solve problems that were exclusively Mexican American. One of these problems was a lack of voice in the city council. CSO made it possible for Edward Roybal to be the first Mexican American elected to the Los Angeles City Council.

In Corpus Christi, Texas, another group began in 1948. The American G. I. Forum was a response to other veterans' organizations which would not allow Mexican Americans to become members. The incident that led to its formation was the refusal of a cemetery in Corpus Christi to bury a Mexican American veteran. MAPA (Mexican American Political Association) began in California. As a political group it offered support to those who promised to help the Mexican American. In Texas a similar group was PASSO (Political Association of Spanish Speaking Organizations).

In all, Mexican Americans were refusing to accept any form of discrimination. Mexican American lawyers fought for equal rights in the courts. Mexican American teachers worked for change within the schools. Remembering their own difficult experiences with the two languages, they asked that Spanish be taught in *barrio* schools, and that the culture and heritage of the Mexican American should also be brought into the classroom. They wanted Mexican Americans to know about themselves all that has been written in this book—and much more.

Little by little, the Mexican Americans developed political power. Politicians sensed the development of this new strength. Those running for office began to heed what was happening in the *barrios* and to cultivate the Mexican American vote. Most of these men were sincere in promising to change things for the better, although some of them merely sought support. Increasingly, Mexican Americans acquired success in gaining political positions, too.

The rising awareness of the Mexican American led to broadening of opportunities. Some Mexican Americans began to find status in areas where no Mexican American had ever before been allowed. Certain government jobs became available for the first time. Banks, insurance companies, businesses of all kinds regularly hired Mexican Americans. Industry began to allow them to advance beyond low-skill jobs. But as yet few high-level jobs were available to them.

Much of this awareness came about as a direct result of the Civil Rights Movement, a series of actions by various minority groups to establish their equal rights. The Blacks took the lead for their conflict embraced the whole nation. Although Mexican Americans also live in all parts of the United States, the majority are in the Southwest, and their numbers are few in comparison to the Black population. Civil rights activity led to the development of government programs, some of them concerned with the problem of poverty. The War On Poverty program established by President Lyndon Johnson called for an all-out government effort to reduce the level of poverty in the United States. It was a program relevant to the Mexican American; in 1964, over one-third of them were living on less than $3,000 a year. Over 80% of employed Mexican Americans had low paying, semi-skilled or unskilled jobs.

Government-sponsored investigations to expose discrimination made it clear that the Mexican American had truly been forgotten by his fellow Americans. He suffered from an inferior education and a low standard of health. The Mexican American infant mortality rate, for example, was much higher than that of the Anglo American. Studies showed for every Anglo American who was without work there were two unemployed Mexican Americans.

Strong-voiced leaders from the Mexican American community demanded the basic American right of equal opportunity. Some were bloodied veterans of the struggle such as Ernesto Galarza, George Sanchez and Julian Samora. Others were new, but equally determined. Most carried the support of organizations. In Texas, there was Alfredo Hernandez who had the support of LULAC. Dr. Miguel Montes, in California, had LACA (Latin American Civic Association). Albert Peña had PASSO. Agustín Flores had the

G. I. Forum. Other men had the general support of all the aware community, as did Dr. Julian Nava in Los Angeles when he won his race for the Board of Education. It was no small victory for Los Angeles is the second largest school district in the nation.

The pressure brought about other changes. Some Mexican Americans were appointed to high ranking positions in the government. Raul H. Castro was appointed ambassador to El Salvador. Dr. Hector García was made a member of the United States delegation to the United Nations. Armando Rodriguez was named Coordinator of the Education Program for the Spanish-speaking. Vicente T. Ximenes was chosen as chairman of the President's Cabinet Committee on Mexican American Affairs. Though in recent years others have been advanced to important positions, these men named here were among the first.

State, county and city governments also felt the pressure and began to place Mexican Americans in positions of responsibility. Some communities elected Mexican Americans to office for the first time in their history. The number of Mexican Americans moving into offices of power and influence have been few. California stands as an example: It is estimated that Mexican Americans comprise about 16% of the state's population. Mexican Americans hold less than 2% of the jobs supported by state funds. One reality to bear in mind is that the Mexican American is a minority not everyone is aware of.

In labor, reforms and reconstruction continued their forward movement. More Mexican Americans became labor union leaders and organizers. Mexican American workingmen experienced a new sense of dignity. For more than 100 years their labor had built up the great industries of the Southwest. Mexican American "sweat" had advanced the agriculture of California, Arizona, New Mexico, Texas and southern Colorado. Their skill had made the cattle and sheep industries possible. Their arms and backs had lifted the rails and maintained the railroads that tied the nation together. Long is the list of industries and projects that have been made possible by the muscle of the Mexican American. Such a history of hard work well deserves their sense of pride and worth. Their labor and know-how still contribute to the growth and development of the United States.

All people of this nation should respect their fellow Americans who have given so much and received so little in return. They have given their sweat and strength, their lives and blood. They have brought beauty and grace and richness. They have contributed chapters of history and a heritage that belong to the whole nation.

It is at this point that we find the Mexican American today. The Mexican American communities have placed their hope for fulfillment in their youth.

PART II — THE MEXICAN AMERICAN TODAY— THE CHICANO GENERATION

Advocates of La Raza

Mexican American youth has injected new vigor into the demand for change, although their philosophy and tactics are not always accepted by everyone in the community. Youth's commitment is to *la raza,* the people. Mexican Americans so committed call themselves *Chicanos.*

The origin of the name *Chicano* is not truly known. Many explanations exist for it, some quite technical. What is generally known is that *Chicano* originally carried an insulting connotation and was used to describe the lowest, the worst of the Mexican people. That youth would seek out such a term to describe themselves is most significant, for it indicates their refusal to accept being changed over, to take on an identity not really their own.

Chicanos question members of previous generations who gave up their identity in order to achieve success. They see the giving up of traditions, customs and language as a "cop-out." *Chicanos* feel pride in being of *mestizo* heritage. The brownness of their skin is a mark of distinction. The ability to express themselves in two languages enriches their power of communication. *Chicanos* stress that the United States is made up of many cultures and that no group should be made to give up its identity. Some cannot for they are visibly distinct.

What is to happen to those whose visibility denies them the choice of shedding or maintaining their identity? Rodolfo "Corky" Gonzales, an active *Chicano* leader from Denver, describes the dilemma in his epic poem, "I Am Joaquin":

I Am Joaquin

I am Joaquin
Lost in a world of confusion
Caught up in a whirl of an
             Anglo society,
Confused by the rules,
Scorned by attitudes,
Suppressed by manipulations,
And destroyed by modern society.
My fathers
       have lost the economic battle
and won
       the struggle of cultural survival.

And now!
   I must choose
       between
  the paradox of
Victory of the spirit,
despite physical hunger
      or
to exist in the grasp
of American social neurosis,
sterilization of the soul
   and a full stomach.
Yes,
   I have come a long way to nowhere,
   unwillingly dragged by that
   monstrous, technical
   industrial giant called
      Progress
an Anglo success . . .
   I look at myself.
   I watch my brothers.
   I shed tears of sorrow.
   I sow seeds of hate.
I withdraw to the safety within the
Circle of life . . .
   My Own People
 . . . .
   La Raza!
Mejicano!
   Español!
     Latino!
      Hispano!
      Chicano!
or whatever I call myself,
   I look the same
   I feel the same
   I cry
     and
   Sing the same.
I am the masses of my people and
I refuse to be absorbed. . . .

The poet clearly shows what today's Mexican American is feeling. He is the new group, the *Chicano* generation. The *Chicano* will not withdraw into the *barrio*, to continue the patterns of the generations before him. He will change the self-image that Mexican Americans have held for so long. He will not stand for seeing himself as cheap labor, or as a person set apart because of his appearance, or as an alien because he speaks Spanish or English with a Spanish accent. The *Chicano* has come to know and understand his heritage in the Southwest, in Aztlán.

This new feeling has created gaps between the generations. It has forced people to choose a course of action. Many older people have elected to support the young. By joining the *Chicano* Movement, they establish themselves as part of the greater community, not as a group living in a *barrio* on the edge of town.

The history of the *Chicano* Movement begins in the era spanning the late 40's to the mid-50's when veterans, at first from World War II, then later from the Korean War, swelled the ranks of those working for change. Their force was strongly felt in the movement to give the Mexican American equal opportunities in all areas of society. *Chicanos* started to be heard more often, more loudly, more clearly.

The Movement developed greater political muscle. New organizations came into being. New leaders came forward. They planned and also held nationwide demonstrations against poverty, and carried out protests in the vital states of the Southwest. Political figures on the national scene, such as President John F. Kennedy and Senator Robert F. Kennedy, became interested and pledged their support. The new pride of the Mexican Americans affected other areas of American society. Entertainers, sports figures, businessmen and actors gave added emphasis to their Mexican American identity.

In Tierra Amarilla, in northern New Mexico, a group of Mexican Americans engaged in an active protest against the United States government. Their leader, Reis Tijerina, demanded the release of land rightfully claimed by his people and neighbors. Through his organization, the *Alianza Federal de Mercedes* (Federal Alliance of Land Grants), Tijerina denounced the government of the United States for cheating them out of the land. With the reclaimed lands, Tijerina planned to establish a free city-state. The lands demanded by the *Alianza* were being used by the government mainly as national forests.

On June 5, 1967, Reis Tijerina led a raid on the County Court House in Tierra Amarilla. His purpose was to make a citizen's arrest on the district attorney, an act he felt he had legal reason to perform, since the district attorney had failed to investigate and make charges regarding the *Alianza's* demands. The raid resulted in some shooting. When it was over, Reis Tijerina and eighteen of his friends were charged with injuring three officers and holding two as hostages. In the trial that followed, Reis Tijerina, acting as his own defense lawyer, was released from all charges.

The raid and the trial drew national attention to the issue of land grants. *Chicanos* and Mexican Americans supported Reis Tijerina, and other Americans began to look more closely at the history of the land grant and the injustices done to the Mexicans during the 1850's.

In the spring of 1969, Tijerina attempted to make a citizen's arrest on three high-ranking officials; Chief Justice of the Supreme Court Warren Burger, Governor David Cargo of New Mexico, and the chief officer of the Los Alamos Scientific Laboratories. Again Tijerina was arrested before he could carry out his plan. This time he did not gain an acquittal and has recently been released from prison.

One thing is perfectly distinct in the actions of Reis Tijerina; although many disapprove of his methods, the people have discovered a *leader,* a hero. *Rey Tigre* (King Tiger) he is called by his admirers. A *corrido* is one of the highest and most honored tributes given by Mexican Americans. The actions of the *Alianza* have inspired the one translated below:

Ballad of Rio Arriba

The year was nineteen sixty-seven,
June fifth was the day,
It was a revolution
There in Tierra Amarilla.

The place was a courthouse
In the town of Tierra Amarilla,
In the state of New Mexico
In the county of Rio Arriba.

A group of our own people
Very unhappily came down,
And on the officers of the state,
They took their sad revenge.

Their leader pleaded with them,
"Don't use any violence!"
But he could not control them
For they had lost their patience.

One deputy there on the floor
Lies wounded, aching with pain,
With a bullet deep in his chest,
There in Tierra Amarilla.

All of the women and children
Rushed away, running and crying.
They thought in that terrible moment,
That everything they had was dying.

Thirty of the men were able
To escape up to the mountain.
And the governor made his call
To the National Guard servicemen.

When they all were captured,
To the prison they were taken
In order that they would be tried
For the crime they were charged with.

This corrido will end
When justice will be done.
In that way no one will have to repeat
What happened in Tierra Amarilla.

Cesar Chavez and Huelga

Another important man has distinguished himself in the eyes of his people. Outwardly, he is no *tigre*. But his dedication, effort and sacrifice have made him a *gigante* (giant). He is Cesar Chavez, a giant among men not only in the fields and backroads of the agricultural land, but also in the *barrios,* the living rooms, the conference rooms, and the halls of Congress.

This mild, gentle man has stated that, "I am convinced that the truest act of courage, the strongest act of manliness, is to sacrifice ourselves for others in a totally non-violent struggle for justice." And so he has.

Cesar Chavez was born in 1927. Not many years later he was toiling in the fields beside his parents. The Chavez family were migrants. They had owned a small farm in Arizona, but had lost it soon after the Depression. Home for Cesar Chavez became a series of cars and tents. He learned at an early age what it was to be without shoes in winter and to eat whatever could be gotten cheap or free. He also learned early about the *coyotes* and their practices.

Needless to say, Cesar Chavez had a hit-and-miss school education. Yet he did manage by the age of fourteen to complete eight years of school before being forced to work fulltime in the fields.

Cesar Chavez married young and raised a family of eight. He left the migrant trails and settled down in San José, California. Mostly he worked the fields during the harvest season, but he also held down other kinds of jobs in town. While living in San José, he became involved in the farm workers' labor movement.

Chavez had always been committed to man's right to be a man. As a teenager he confronted segregation in a movie house. He had been asked to move to the "Mexican section" of the theater because he looked Mexican. Only fifteen years old, Cesar refused and was thrown out. Shortly after, he joined the National Farm Labor Union and marched in the picket lines.

The turning point in his life occurred while he was living in the *barrio* of San José, *Sal-si-puedes* (Get-out-if-you-can). Here he came into contact with the parish priest, Father Donald McDonnell. Father McDonnell opened up a new world to Cesar Chavez. Life, he learned, could be something better, even for a former migrant. Chavez also learned that the first move in helping the farm workers was getting them to unite. A strong symbolic force among the Mexican farmworkers was the Virgin of Guadalupe, the "Brown Madonna," who has figured significantly in the lives of Mexicans since her first appearance nearly 400 years ago, in Mexico. This religious symbol played an important role in Cesar Chavez' early work and continued to help him in later years.

The second highlight in the making of Cesar Chavez was his encounter with Fred Ross of the Community Service Organization (CSO). Ross was a professional organizer who had become a part of CSO in the years immediately following World War II. Ross was hired to train the Mexican American population to organize East Los Angeles. There his success can be partly measured in Edward Roybal's election to the Los Angeles City Council. Fred Ross moved from one Mexican American community to another helping the people to organize CSO chapters. In 1952 he arrived in San José, where he met Cesar Chavez.

What Chavez learned from Ross fitted in with what he had learned from Father McDonnell. It was not long before Cesar Chavez became a CSO organizer himself. At first he found his role difficult because he is a shy, modest man to whom leadership has not come easily. The CSO offered to the people of the *colonias* and *barrios* a way of solving their problems. It offered them a way to fight being displaced by *braceros*. Cesar Chavez became a state-wide organizer of the CSO.

The CSO won many battles, but failed to defeat the *bracero* program. Finally, a majority of CSO people suggested that all Mexican Americans pull out of agricultural work, leaving that area of work strictly to the *bracero*. Chavez did not agree. He insisted that the *bracero* program itself must end. Farm work should be upgraded so that people would not look down on those who labored in the fields.

The CSO would not support Chavez' thinking. Aften ten years of work with the organization, he resigned. Leaving San José, he moved in 1962 to Delano in the San Joaquin Valley of California to organize the agricultural workers of the rich grape industry. There he formed the Farm Workers Association, a name later changed to the National Farm Workers Association.

Cesar Chavez put into practice the best teachings of Fred Ross and Father McDonnell. He stressed their idea that people with common problems must band together in an organized group and come to solutions themselves. Believing this with his whole heart, Cesar Chavez refused help from major organizations, for he feared that all such help would create unwanted obligations for his people. Not until the FWA was well formed did he accept outside help.

The years that followed were hard. The members of FWA suffered greatly for their effort. Most could not even afford the dues. But they stayed together, thanks to the efforts of Cesar

Chavez. Every night, after working in the fields all day, he went out on his organizing rounds, constantly increasing FWA membership. Organizing was difficult and expensive. Nearly all the Chavez family worked in the fields to make ends meet. Cesar Chavez set an example for all the FWA members. And because the people believed in him, they followed.

At first the efforts of FWA were directed to small problems. Their success served to give the group a feeling of accomplishment. By 1964, the Association had about 1,000 dues-paying members. By 1965, they were large enough to attack some major problems, winning each of their fights. FWA glowed with a real feeling of success and a measure of its strength. The real test of power came in late summer of that year.

The *bracero* program had come to an end on December 31, 1964. Nevertheless, the United States government allowed card-carrying Mexican labor to cross the border. The law required that this labor receive $1.40 per hour, a rate higher than that being paid to American farm workers.

In May, in the Coachella Valley of Southern California, another table grape center, Filipino agricultural workers went on strike, demanding $1.40 an hour. The grape growers gave in to their union, the AWOC (Agriculture Workers Organizing Committee), a victory that was to last as long as the work continued. In September, table grapes were ready for harvest around Delano. Many of the Filipino migrant workers moved to Delano for that harvest, fully expecting to be paid the $1.40 rate. The growers offered $1.20, plus a bonus of five cents per man per box. The Filipinos again went on strike through the AWOC.

The question now was whether the FWA would support the Filipino workers. If they did not, would they be acting as strike breakers? The decision was a hard one. The FWA was not very strong. Cesar Chavez was not sure they could successfully undertake a strike. Yet how could they continue to work while their brother workers suffered? A meeting was called on September 16 (the day Mexico celebrates its independence from Spain). Chavez pointed out to the members the realities of strike conditions. The families would certainly undergo hardships for the FWA did not have enough money or power to protect its members. Yet when a vote was taken the unanimous choice was for *huelga* (strike).

This *huelga* was different from any other strike that had ever taken place in the San Joaquin Valley. The pickets were not aggressive and violence was rejected. The strikers carried along with their flags and symbols a banner showing the Virgin of Guadalupe, the "Brown Madonna."

Soon the press picked up the story of this unusual strike, bringing attention to the many problems of the farmworker. The Spanish word *huelga* became familiar the country over. The strikers were joined by religious leaders, students, citizens from all walks of life. Many came to work with the strikers, others to give only token support. The feeling was that the strike would not last. But it went on month after month.

The strike began to create complications. It involved many millions and millions of dollars, many major industries, and other unions as well. The issues were taken directly to the California capital. The strikers followed, marching 230 miles from Delano to Sacramento carrying before them the "Brown Madonna." The march attracted even more attention to the cause of the strikers. Hundreds joined the strikers as they marched into the Sacramento capitol.

The following *corrido* was written for that march:

El Corrido de Cesar Chavez

One day, the seventh of March,
Holy Thursday in the morning,
Cesar left Delano
Organizing a campaign.

"Farmworking companions,
This will be an example,
This march we're taking
To the very center of Sacramento."

When we arrived in Fresno,
All the people were yelling,
"Long live Cesar Chavez!"
And the people he was leading.

We bade farewell to Fresno,
We bade farewell with faith,
In order to arrive happily
Up to the town of Merced.

We're now arriving in Stockton;
The sun has almost set.
But my people go on yelling,
"Continue with lots of faith."

When we arrived in Stockton,
The *mariachis* were playing.
"Long live Cesar Chavez!
And the Virgin that he's taking."

Contractors and scabs,
This is going to be the story
Of your going to hell
And our going to glory.

That Mr. Cesar Chavez,
He is a perfect man,
He wants to be face to face
With Governor Brown.

Listen, Mr. Cesar Chavez,
You, whose name resounds,
On your chest you deserve
The Virgin of Guadalupe!

Chavez held fast, while the growers wavered. Avoiding a decision, they apparently wanted to wait out the strikers. But the pressure was on; they could not afford to wait for they had too much at stake. In the camps where the strikers stayed, there was a great deal of misery and sorrow. Cesar Chavez had the difficult job of keeping up the strikers' spirits. At this important time, Chavez was suffering terribly from a back ailment and was in constant pain.

As the strike dragged on, one change had to be made. In order to appear unanimous and powerful, the FWA and the AWOC had to unite. On August 22, 1966, they merged into the United Farm Workers Organizing Committee (UFWOC) AFL–CIO. Cesar Chavez became director, and the head of AWOC, the assistant director. The new union took as its symbol a black thunderbird on a red background.

What followed was a long trail of pickets, boycotts, marches and endless fund-raising activities. The details are complex and are best left to be recorded in books dedicated to that subject alone. What is important to include here is an appreciation for the people who fought so hard against such terrible odds, and won.

Cesar Chavez led his workers to victory, but the fight took a great deal out of him. To fight without the use of force or violence is one of the hardest of all battles. For it requires that one fight against himself first. It is not easy to accept insult, pain, abuse without wanting to return it in kind. At times, he voluntarily suffered more than his followers, for he wished to show them that he understood their burden. This *gigante,* Cesar Chavez, continues to show the way, for the battles are not over.

Equally important is what Cesar Chavez has done for all the Mexican American community. He has demonstrated that it is possible to create understanding and awareness. He has proved it does not have to be done through violence.

Community Organizations

The year 1967 was important in the Mexican American community for it marked the beginning of other major activities. In October, President Lyndon Johnson called for a special investigation at El Paso, Texas, the Cabinet Committee Hearings on Mexican American Affairs. It was a response to pressure from various community organizations. The community wanted the hearings to be held in the White House. When El Paso was selected as the hearing place, many *Chicanos* were annoyed. Those who refused to go formed their own committee of investigation. They called themselves *La Raza Unida* Conference (The United People's Conference), and met in the *barrio* of El Paso. This group claimed the Cabinet Committee Hearings were nothing but a political move to gain support for the group in power.

The four cabinet members presiding at the Cabinet Committee Hearings on Mexican American Affairs received a message from *La Raza Unida* Conference. The government hearings would lead to nothing because no evidence showed that the government was sincere. As proof of sincerity, the government should have made reforms before calling the hearings. Further, in order to bring national attention to the problems of the Mexican American, it should have held the hearings in the White House.

Among the leaders of *La Raza Unida* Conference were Ernesto Galarza and Rodolfo "Corky" Gonzales of Denver, Colorado. The Conference was a sort of prelude to a new political party, *La Raza Unida* Party. *La Raza Unida* Party supports only those political candidates who hold high the interest of the Mexican American. The party has already played a major role in elections in Texas and California. Its power presently comes through its being able to split the vote; therefore, it can cause a candidate to lose.

The activities in Texas led to action in other areas. The students began to organize. Their main purposes were first, to support the actions of groups like *La Raza Unida* and second, to make changes in the education of the Mexican American in the public schools.

MAYO (Mexican American Youth Organization) was organized in Texas. College campuses saw the rise of other organizations, such as UMAS (United Mexican American Students) and MASC (Mexican American Studies Confederation). These groups worked hard at getting Mexican American studies programs established on the various campuses. As the organizations grew so did the *Chicano* Movement. The students began to develop a fresh feeling about themselves. They wanted no compromise to their identity. The feeling of being *Chicano* strengthened and solidified. By 1969, many UMAS groups came together as MECHA (*Movimiento Estudiantíl Chicano de Aztlán*) (Chicano Student Movement of Aztlán). This step was a major one. In many cases, MECHA made a break with the established ways of the *barrio*. It placed outstanding importance on the *mestizo* culture, especially the Indian aspect of it. The students had that feeling about themselves described at the beginning of this section.

Student action spread throughout the Southwest/Aztlán. Students walked out of their classes. The first such walkout in the Los Angeles City Schools took place in April, 1968. The walkout was to bring attention to their problems. Students called for the schools to teach in two languages, Spanish and English. The pressures of their demands drew national attention. A Senate investigation group had already recommended passage of a bill encouraging two-language (bilingual) teaching by providing funds. That bill became law in 1967, but only $7,500,000 was granted, an amount that could never take care of the millions of bilingual students in the United States.

Students continued to demonstrate. In 1969 *Chicano* students walked out for nine days in Abilene, Texas. Most students did not attend school during December of that year in Crystal City, Texas. *Chicano* students have walked out in Denver and other communities throughout the five Southwestern states. Although these walkouts have brought some national concern, changes are slow in coming.

Lately, the government has responded to the appeals to provide equal opportunities for members of minority groups. One attempt has been to help minority youth to go to college. Some colleges which a few years ago had only forty Mexican American students, now show an enrollment of 1,500 or more.

These students differ from most college students in terms of their reasons for going to college. They have promised themselves to return to their *barrios* after college. They want to educate the young. They want to make contributions. They want to increase pride in their heritage. They want the differences that mark them from the Anglo Americans to be accepted by all. Their commitment promises that the work and contributions of many Mexican Americans will be recognized and respected. In many ways, they go to college not for themselves alone, but for *la raza*.

The students join the Mexican Americans in calling themselves *Chicanos*. In political campaigns they provide the "leg work" and leaflets to support their selected leaders. They help Cesar Chavez by raising money and gathering food and clothing for the striking farmworkers. *Chicanos* are dedicated. They donate many hours as tutors for *Chicano* school children. They work in rehabilitation programs for former drug addicts. They teach classes in penal institutions. They counsel high school students and other young people in trouble. They represent *la raza* in committees, panels and community action. They organize demonstrations against agencies or groups that they consider unfair or unjust to Mexican Americans.

The activities of the *Chicanos* and other Mexican American groups have developed other forms of expression. The media of literature and art serve as outlets for creative feelings. Various kinds of original, exciting, and moving poetry and prose are being written. These works appear in magazines, anthologies, and as individual novels. Theater groups are presenting original dramas by young Mexican American playwrights. Some of these authors first began their careers in farm worker camps, where they wrote plays to entertain the farm workers who were on strike. One such group is the *Teatro Campesino* (The Farmworkers Theater). Other artists create paintings, sculpture, and pottery. Their work is often on exhibit, and numerous pieces have become part of permanent collections of fine colleges and museums. Dance groups present traditional folk dances alongside dances that reflect the happenings in the community. Newspapers, magazines, journals, and other publications are pouring out of the *barrios*. These publications inform, entertain, and stimulate pride in the heritage of the Mexican American.

Any activity that may lead to change has always received many kinds of reactions. Some of the reactions may end in violence. That ending has stamped a few of the marches setting out from the *barrios*. These marches have been demonstrations of protest against war, unfair police controls, bad treatment of farm workers, and similar crises. When marches have met with active resistance, the result has been violence and death.

In Los Angeles on August 29, 1970, Ruben Salazar was the victim of a tragedy. Salazar was killed in the violence that followed a peaceful march in protest of the war in Viet Nam. This newspaper reporter and TV commentator had been a strong voice for the Mexican American people. Ruben Salazar's death also created a new type of unity. Mexican Americans who had never before been active joined groups to work out peaceful methods of protest.

Peaceful methods such as those used by Cesar Chavez are often the preferred way to effect change. This thinking is not easy for all to accept. Many young people are furious and impatient. To these young *Chicanos,* the change is too slow in coming. They look back in anger at the century and a half of being ignored and forgotten. Some *Chicanos* have organized groups that call for immediate forceful action. One such group was the Brown Berets. This group raised its voice loudly in attempting reforms. It received encouragement from a number of Mexican Americans. Members of the Brown Berets triggered the action in *barrios* where little or nothing was happening. They stimulated the Mexican American movement to achieve equal opportunity. When community disapproval marked their military organization and tactics, the Brown Berets disbanded, their members joining various more acceptable groups.

Dynamic changes are taking place in the Mexican American community. In addition to an outpouring of literature and art, the community has developed an intellectual character. A person can be wholly identified as Chicano in terms of appearance, creative ability, and intellect. This *Chicano* is no longer bound by the *barrio* or *colonia,* but moves at ease on the university campus, is a force in law and politics, and an influential activist in such popular movements as Women's Lib, Bilingual Education, and Cultural Democracy.

The words *carnalismo, la causa,* and *el movimiento* are keys to the meaning of the Chicano individuality. *Carnalismo* means, loosely, "brotherhood," but in a literal sense it means "flesh of my flesh," a reflection of the indigenous origins of the Mexican American. *Carnalismo* suggests the knowledge that all humans are alike because they share the same parents—mother-Earth and father-Sky. *La causa,* an expression that fits well in the American scene, translates as "the cause," an expression that has been used by many groups of Americans to designate their fight against oppression. To the *Chicano* it signifies the combat for dignity. *El movimiento* means "the movement," all those who are involved in bettering the lot of the Mexican American. *El movimiento* has as its basis those principles the United States is committed to; those principles set forth by the revolutionary leaders who fought against domination by Great Britain.

Other developments include the establishment of an intellectual center that emphasizes the indigenous elements of the make-up of the *mestizo*. D-Q University, DQU, was founded in California in 1970. According to Jack D. Forbes, one of the outstanding contributors to the University's growth, the "D" signifies a sacred name—the Peacemaker. The Peacemaker was the founder of the Iroquois union of nations before the Europeans came to the Americas. The "Q" stands for Quetzalcoatl, the spirit in Mexican mythology who created human life. Quetzalcoatl also was a Toltec leader who made major changes among the Mexican people a thousand years ago. This leader is generally pictured in indigenous Mexican art and architecture as a plumed serpent.

There is also increased participation by the Mexican American community in programs that deal with the health, vitality, and education of its very young, its aged, its handicapped, and its gifted. The community is aggressively seeking out those material means that will support programs and projects for improving the life of all of its people.

Equally important is the modification of attitude and action in the surrounding larger community which has gained a growing appreciation of its fellow citizens.

Real progress takes more than awareness. There must be acceptance and understanding. There must be respect. As Benito Juarez, a president of Mexico, said: *"El respeto al derecho ajeno es la paz"* ("Peace is respect for the rights of others").

As this book is written, the Southwest rings with names of leaders such as Cesar Chavez, Reis Tijerina, Ernesto Galarza, "Corky" Gonzales, Elegio de la Garza, Leopoldo Sanchez, Hank Lopez, Manuel Ramirez, Rudy Acuña, and scores of others. Sounding also are the as yet unheard names of young *Chicanos* and Mexican Americans, who are working to make all people who belong to that part of the United States, called the Southwest/ Aztlán, into one people.

SUGGESTED ACTIVITIES

Chapter I—The Seven Cities of Cíbola

1. Seek out mythical tales about strange exotic lands such as Shangri-La, Atlantis, Camelot, El Dorado.
2. Investigate other explorers who have gone into the unknown. What were their hardships? Some examples are Perry, Livingston, Byrd, Polo, Glenn, Lindbergh, Cook.
3. What other slaves or former slaves made major contributions to history? What motivated them? Consider Spartacus, Carver, Douglass, Sojourner Truth, Malinche.
4. Make a detailed map of the area covered by Fray Marcos and Esteban. Put a transparent overlay on the map. On the overlay show the area as it is today, including such features as roads, railroad lines, major government projects, cities, etc.
5. Research some of the lore and tales of the Hopi, Zuñi, Navajo, Apache, and other Indian nations of Aztlán.
6. Research the types of weaponry and armor used by the Spaniards in the 15th and 16th centuries.
7. Research and sketch examples of Indian pottery, weaving, art and crafts, religious objects, and other artifacts that date back to the 16th and 17th centuries. Compare them with the art and crafts produced by the same Indians today.

Chapter II—Gold and God

1. Compare the founding and colonization of Jamestown and Santa Fe.
2. Read *Death Comes for the Archbishop* by Willa Cather. How much of the novel is based on real people, on the Uprising of 1680 in New Mexico?
3. Trace the development of the horse. What breeds of horses were brought to the New World? What breeds have been developed in the New World? Include in your study the donkey and the mule.
4. Make a chart of the systems of control used by the Spanish in all their colonies: the Church, the military, the civil. Where did they overlap? Compare these systems of government with the British system in the New World.
5. Write a dialogue between Juan de Oñate and John Smith in which they discuss their colonies.
6. Select four different Indian nations, from four different parts of the United States, and compare them in regard to dress, clothing, customs dealing with marriage, death, child rearing,

old age, political organization, and religious traditions. Limit your research to the period during which they made their first contacts with the white man.

Chapter III—Northward Movement

1. Considering the work of Father Kino and the effect it had upon the Indians he contacted, evaluate the constructive and the destructive aspects of missionary work.
2. What major events were taking place in India and China at the time of the founding of the missions in California?
3. Research the life and customs of the *Californios*. Follow this research with the reading of some of the romantic novels set in California before the arrival of the Anglo Americans.
4. Make a detailed study of Russia's activities in the New World. What prompted the Russians to attempt colonization in the New World? Who, were some of the main personalities involved? What was the eventual outcome of these efforts?
5. Prepare a report of French activities in Louisiana. How did the Revolution of 1792 in France affect the French colonies? What effect did the rise of Napoleon have on the colonies?
6. Do a careful study of the Mississippi River System. How would the absence of this river system affect the United States? How would the course of history have been changed if there had not been a Mississippi River?

Chapter IV—A New Culture

1. Where else in the world have people mixed to create *mestizo* (mixed-blood) people? How are these people accepted in the larger community? What problems have these people had to face? Some examples are Eurasians, Hawaiians, Cubans, Jamaicans.
2. Make a collection of simple decorative artifacts in common use today. In report form, point out the various influences that are easily visible in them, such as design, shape, color, material, and so forth. (Some of these artifacts may be vases, bowls, rugs, tapestries.)
3. Search out Indian works that tell the story about the coming of the white man. One good source is *The Broken Spears, the Aztec Account of the Conquest of Mexico*, ed. Miguel Leon Portilla, Boston: Beacon Press. Do the same for other cultures.
4. Study the myths and legends of various Indian groups of Mexico and the American Southwest, such as the Yaqui, the Apache, the Maya.

Chapter V—Strangers from the East

1. Research the background of General James Wilkinson and his association with Manifest Destiny.
2. What are some of the documents or writings that tell about human rights? Compare the various writings, noting the differences in time and authorship.
3. Search out a map that will show the various land grants made to Anglo Americans in *Tejas*. What land grants are made by the United States government today?
4. What happened in other Spanish colonies during the time Spain was invaded by Napoleon (1807- 1818)? Who were some of the personalities involved?
5. What events in Florida led to the Florida Treaty? What role did the Seminole Indians play in this treaty?
6. Using Cecil Robinson's *With the Ears of Strangers* (University of Arizona Press, 1969), read excerpts from the writings of other mountain men who lived in or visited the Southwest. Discuss the role of literature in creating false ideas about people, places, events.
7. Read various reports on Texas' war for independence and compare them. (See *The Republic of Texas,* ed. Stephen B. Oates, American West Publishing Company, 1968.)

Chapter VI—The Southwest

1. Read Glenn W. Price's *Origins of the War with Mexico* (University of Texas Press, 1967) and compare it with other accounts.
2. Study in detail the Treaty of Guadalupe Hidalgo. What are the conditions of payment of the stated $15,000,000? What are the guarantees given to Mexicans? How are Indians provided for? What does the Treaty say about Indian slaves? What is the language that describes the boundaries?
3. Where else in the world has the discovery of precious metals or jewels or vital resources caused great rushes?
4. Make a map locating the various Indian reservations of the Southwest. Draw some conclusions regarding their locations.
5. Study some of the great irrigation projects of the world, e.g., Egypt, Greece, People's Republic of China, U.S.S.R., United States.

Chapter VII—The Mexican American

For additional reading—

    "Huelgistas" a play from Luis Valdez'
        Teatro Campesino
    "Aztecs del Norte," Jack Forbes

"Barrio Boy," Ernesto Galarza
"Papa and Pancho Villa," Enrique "Hank" Lopez
"So Shall You Reap, The Story of Cesar Chavez and
     The Farm Workers' Movement," Joan London and Henry
     Anderson
"Delano, The Story of the California Grape Strike,"
     John Gregory Dunne
"Macho!", Edmund Villasenor
"I am JoaquinYo Soy Joaquin," Rodolfo Gonzales
"People of the Valley," Frank Waters
"El Grito," Quinto Sol Publications, Inc.

Index

Acaxee, 18
Acoma (Sky City of Acoma, *also* Holy City of), 12, 21, 36, 40, 48
agricultural industry, 78, 129, 140, 143, 149-152, 164; *agribusiness*, 149-152
Agricultural Workers Organizing Committee (AWOC), 165
Alarcón, Hernando de, 12, 20
alcalde, 17, 77, 81
Alianza Federal de Mercedes (Federal Alliance of Land Grants), 160
Alvarado, Governor, 97
Alvarado, Pedro de, 15-17, 25, 26
Anza, Don Juan Baptista de, 58, 63
Apache, 18, 23, 24, 43, 44, 47, 49, 50, 56, 57, 68, 78, 80, 96, 115, 119, 121-126, 137
architecture, 22, 25, 65, 71, 72, 91, 92
Armijo, Antonio, 96
audiencia, 81
Austin, Stephen F., 90, 101

Baja California (Lower California), 15, 34, 51-53, 55, 58
the *barrio*, 135, 136, 139, 140, 145, 153, 159, 160, 162-164, 168-171
Bent, Governor Charles, 108
bijuela, 76
Bilingual education, 169, 171
Border Wars, 104, 105, 136-139
Bowie, James, 96, 100
braceros, 149-152, 164, 165
Brown Berets, 171

Cabeza de Vaca, Alvar Nuñez, 7-9, 12, 15, 16, 26, 28, 31
Caddo, 18
Calafía, 7, 15
California Indians, 61, 62, 65, 78
Californios, 88, 89, 96, 104, 109, 111-114, 117-119, 127
Campo, Andrés de, 28
Cardenas, Garcia Lopez de, 21
Carson, Kit, 95, 111
Causa, La, 171

cattle ranching, 55, 76, 77, 90, 95, 112, 127, 129, 141, 157
Chaco Canyon, 22
Chavez, Cesar, 151, 152, 162-168, 171
Cherokee, 100
Chicano, 158-160, 169-171; movement, 160, 161
Chihuahua Trail, 131
Cíbola, Seven Cities of, 6, 7, 10-15, 17, 18, 20, 28, 30, 35
Cicuye (Pecos), 22, 25
Ciudad Juarez, Mexico, 46, 152
Coachella Valley, California, 165
Coahuila, 68
Cochise, 125, 126
Cocopa, 18
Coheta, 18
Coloma, California, 117
colonia, (see barrio), 136, 143, 164
Colorado, 1, 85, 103, 141, 143, 157
Comanches, 24, 49, 68, 78, 123
Community Service Organization (CSO), 155, 163, 164
Confederación de Uniones Obreras Mexicanas (CUOM), 146
conquistador(es), 19, 26, 73, 74, 117
Coronado, Francisco Vasquez de, 13, 17, 31
expedition, 16, 17-22, 25-29, 30-32, 35, 41, 47
Cortez, Hernán, 9, 36, 39
Crespi, Father Juan de, 58, 60
Crockett, David, 101
Culiacán, 7-10, 12, 13, 17, 35
culture; adaptations of, 3, 4; artistic expressions in, 71-76, 125; differences, 44; merging in Pimería Alta, 55, 56; exchange, 98; exchange between Pueblos and Spaniards, 25, 29; of caballero, 18; of Indian warrior, 18, 20; of nomadic Indians, 24, 124, 125; Spanish, 38, 39; Santa Fe, 92-94; rejection of Spanish, 46

Díaz, Melchor, 17, 19-21, 32
Dolores (mission), California, 64
Dolores (mission), Sonora, 52

177

D.Q.U. (D. Quetzalcoatl University), 171
Dorantes, Andrés, 7, 9, 10

El Alamo, 68, 101, 102
El Camino del Diablo, 52
El Camino Real, 90, 96
El Gran Cañon del Río Colorado (the Canyon), 21
El Grito de Dolores, 87, 89
El Paso (del Norte), 42, 46, 47, 50, 76, 81, 115, 122, 136, 152, 154, 168
England; colonies, 70, 83; in Mississippi Valley, 58; visits to California, 66
Escalones, Luis de, 28
Espejo, Antonio de, 35, 36

Fort Hill, 110
Fort Ross, 97
Franciscans, 34, 35, 40, 50, 57, 64, 67, 68
Fremont, John C., 109-111
French exploration, 66, 84; fur trading, 49; in Mississippi Valley, 58; world trade, 69, 83

Gadsden, James, 122; Purchase, 122, 123
Galarza, Dr. Ernesto, 151, 152, 156, 168,171
Gallup, New Mexico, 149
Garces, Father Pedro, 57, 58, 63, 64
gold rush, 117, 127, 130
Gongalez, Rodolfo "Corky," 158, 168
grants; Spanish land, 78, 79; claims, 126-129; encomienda, 78; impresario, 90-100; pueblo, 79; settlement of, 126-129; sitio, 79; and Tijerina, 160-162; to foreigners, 84; in Treaty of Guadalupe-Hidalgo, 116; villas, 79
grapes, 46, 65, 129, 142, 143, 146, 164, 165
greaser, 119, 122, 127, 131, 132, 136, 139, 144
green card carriers, 152, 165
gringos, 110, 119, 122, 131, 132, 136, 137, 139, 144
Guadalajara, 81
Guerrero, Vicente, 89
Guebavi (mission), 54, 57
Gulf of California, 15, 17, 55
Gulf of Mexico, 7, 90

hacendados, 78, 80, 93
haciendas, 46, 78, 92
Hawikuh, 12, 13, 19, 20
hidalgo, 37, 56
Hidalgo, Father Francisco, 67
Hidalgo y Costilla, Miguel, 86, 87, 89
Hohokam, 51
Honorato, Fray de, 10
Hopi, 12, 18, 20, 21, 24, 40; revenge, 48, 49
Houston, Sam, 100-102
huelga (strike), 162, 165, 166
Huichol, 18

Indian (See Acaxee, Apache, Aztec, Caddo, Cherokee, Cocopa, Coheta, Comanche, Cora, Guasave, Hohokam, Hopi, Huichol, Inca, Iroquois, Jumanos, Mayo, Mission Indians, Osage, Paiute, Papago, Pawnee, Pima, Piro, Queres, Tahu, Tehua, Tepihua, Tigrea, Toltec, Totoram, Utes, Wichita, Yaqui, Yuma, Zuni).
Iroquois, 171
irrigation, 2, 3, 24, 56, 129, 130, 141

Jackson, President Andrew, 100
Jefferson, President Thomas, 85
Jesuits, 51, 57
Jornada de la Muerte, 42
Juarez, Presidente Benito, 171
Jumanos, 47

Kearny, Colonel Stephen Watts, 107
Kino, Father Eusebio, 51-56, 58, 63
Kiva, 24, 48

Labor; Black, 141; bracero, 149-151; cheap, 140, 143-145; discrimination in, 147; Ernesto Galarza and, 151; hacienda, 80; hand, 142, 143; importation of, 145; Indian, 42, 43; Mexican, 139-143; migrant, 140-144; Oriental, 143; peonage system of, 80; reforms, 157; strikes, 146, 147; 165; unions, 146, 148, 151, 152, 157; wetback, 150; World War I and, 149, 150; World War II and, 149, 150; working condition of, 144, 148
La Paz, Baja California, 34, 52
La Raza, 158, 170, 171
La Villa Real de la Santa Fe de San Francisco, (See Santa Fe), 41
League of United Latin American Citizens, (LULAC), 154-156
leather craft, 56, 73, 87
Liga Obreras de Habla Español, 148, 149
Limantour, Jose, 127
Lopez, Enrique "Hank," 171
Lopez, Francisco, 117
Lower California, (See Baja California), 15

Mangas, Coloradas, 125
Manifest Destiny, 98, 99, 117, 130
Manila Galleons, 31-33, 53
Matamoros, Mariano, 89
Mayo, 18
Medina, Bartolome de, 120
mejicano, 105
Mesa Verde, 22
mestizo, 2, 3, 36, 38, 39, 50, 56, 65, 71-80, 82, 89, 99, 158, 169
Mexican American, 2, 4, 50, 116, 130, 133, 135-171
Mexican American Political Association, (MAPA), 155

Mexican American Studies Confederation, (MASC), 169
Mexican American Youth Organization, (MAYO), 169
Mexican Independence; first attempt at, 86-89; final struggle for, with Morelos, Matamoros, 165
Mexican Revolution, (1910-1922), 144, 145, 147, 148, 151
Mexican War, (War with the United States), 105-111
Mexico, Republic of, (*Los Estados Unidas de Mexico*), 89, 98
mining, 2, 35, 118-121, 125, 126, 129, 139; *arrastre*, 120; *batea*, 119; dry digging, 120; mining industry law, 121; *patio* process, 121; *placer*, 119
Missions, 58, 60, 62, 65, 68, 76; architecture, 71, 72; changeover from Jesuit to Franciscan control, 57; destruction in 1680, development and economy, 42; in *Alta California*, 58-60; in Pimeriá Alta, 52-55
Mission Indians of California, 65; of *Tejas*, 66-68
Mojaves, 123
Montana, 141
Morelos, Jose Maria, 89
Mormons, 144; Battalion, 115
Movimiento Estudiantil Chicano de Aztlan, (MECHA), 169
Murieta, Joaquin, 132

Nahua, 1, 9; language (Nahuatl), 1, 9
Narvaez, Panfilo, 7, 15
National Agricultural Workers Union, 164
National Farm Labor Union, 163
Navajos, 24, 43, 44, 49, 123, 124
Niza, Fray Marcos de, 10-13, 15-17, 19
Nuestra Señora de Dolores, (mission), 54
Nueva España, 7, 9, 13, 17, 28-30, 32-37, 41, 42, 50, 51, 58, 60, 63, 64, 70, 71, 76, 82, 85-88
Nuevo Mexico, 50; missions in, 60, 61, 71, 85, 86, 91; population in 1750, 50

Old Spanish Trail, 65, 96, 98
Oñate, Don Juan de, 36-38, 40, 41, 79
Ortiz, Juan, 15, 16
Osage Indians, 85

Pachucos, 153, 154
Padilla, Fray Juan de, 22, 28
Paiute, 96
Panuco, (Tampico), 16, 28
Pallares, Jesús, 147-149
Papago, 52, 57, 63
Paredes, Ignacio, 120
Pattie, James Ohio, 95
Pawnee, 18, 25, 85
Pecos, (Cicuye), 22, 25, 28; chiefs, 22, foothills, 28; pueblos, 21, 36; River, 8
peninsulares, 50, 82

peon, 80, 89, 113; peonage system, 80
Pico, Andrés, 111, 114
Pico, Pio, 109, 111
Pike, Zebulon Montgomery, 85, 86
Pima Indians, 11, 18, 51-53, 56, 57
Pimería Alta, 50, 51, 54, 57, 60
Pinda Lick-o-yi (white eyes), 126, 139
Piñeda, Alonso Alvarez de, 6
Piro, 18
Political Associations of Spanish Speaking Organizations, (PASSO), 155, 156
Polk, President James, 105, 109
Popé, 44-47
Portolá, Gaspar de, 58-60
presidio, 58, 60, 63-66, 68, 81, 109
Pueblo Indians, 22-25, 66, 123; adaptation in religion, 38; artistic expression, 23; in Nuevo Mexico, 50; in Mexico, 47-49; irrigation practices, 24, 129; life style, 23; Popé uprising, 43-47, 66; revolt against *Americanos*, 108; Santa Fe, 91, 108; Spanish reconquest of New Mexico, 47-49; tribute labor, 42
pueblo, 11, 15, 21, 26, 37, 49, 91, 108, 128; grants, 79

Queen Calafía, 7, 15
Quetzalcoatl, 171
Queres, 18
quinta, 31, 37, 43, 78, 121
Quivira, 26-28

railroads, 139-142; bracero labor, 150; further expansion, 143; labor, 157; World War I, 145; worker strike, 146
Rangers, (Texas Rangers), 126, 132, 136, 137
Remedios (mission), 54
Republic of Mexico, 98-102, 103-109, 116, 122, 123, 127, 131
Republic of Texas, 105
retablos, 72
Rey Tigre, (Reis Tijerina), 161
Río Grande, (Río del Norte), 8, 22, 26, 28, 35-38, 42, 46, 76, 85, 105, 106, 115, 136, 151
Rodriguez, Fray Agustin, 55

Sacramento, California, 109, 122, 151, 156
Sal-si-puedes, (*barrio*), 136; of San Jose, California, 163
Salt War (of 1877), 136
San Antonio (mission), California, 60
San Antonio de Valero Mission, (El Alamo), 60, 68
San Antonio, Texas, 86, 90, 101, 131, 165
San Diego, California, 34, 59, 60, 63, 95, 111, 115, 116, 154
San Gabriel (mission), California, 60, 63, 64
San Gabriel, Nuevo Mexico, 41, 95, 96
San Idelfonso (pueblo), 43

San Isidro (mission), 53
San Joaquin Valley, California, 64, 97, 146, 164, 165
San Jose, California, 120, 163, 164
San Juan Bautista, New Mexico, 3, 38, 40; colonists, 39, 40
San Juan Bautista (mission), Tejas, 67, 68
San Luis Obispo (mission), California, 60
San Saba Mines, 96
Santa Anna, Antonio Lopez de, 100-103, 122
Santa Cruz (first name for California), 7
Santa Cruz de la Cañada (New Mexico colony), 50
Santa Fe, New Mexico, (La Villa Real de la Santa Fe de San Francisco), 36, 41, 42, 44-50, 69, 71, 86, 91-94, 96, 107, 115
Santa Fe Trail, 90, 91, 94, 96, 131
Santa Rita Mine, New Mexico, 96, 121
santos, 72
San Xavier del Bac (mission), 54, 57
Scott, General Winfield, 107, 115
Serra, Father Junipero, 58-63
Seven Caves of Aztlán, 6, 9
sheep ranching, 73, 76, 77, 92, 129, 139
slavery, 7-10, 25, 40, 43, 50, 80, 90, 96, 99, 100, 125, 131, 139
Sonora, 12, 51-53, 55, 64, 118, 119; River, 12, 20; Altar, 63; mines, 119
Soto, Hernando de, 15, 16, 28
strikes, 146, 147, 165, 167, 170
Sutter, John, 97
Sutter Fort, 109

Tahu, 18
Teatro Campesino (The Farmworkers Theater), 170
Tehua, 18, 44
Tenochtitlán (Mexico City), 1, 9, 19
Tepihuan, 18
Texas (Tejas), 1, 6-8, 16, 27, 35, 47, 50, 69, 76, 88, 89-91, 98-101, 104, 105, 115, 121, 126, 131, 132, 137, 139, 141, 143, 155-157, 168, 169
Texas Rangers, (See Rangers)
Tigrea, 18
Tiguex, 22, 26-28, 35, 36
Tijerina, Reis, 160-162, 171
Toltec, 171
Totonteac, 12, 13
Totoram, 18
Tovar, Pedro de, 20, 21
transportation; routes to California, 122; stage lines, 122; transcontinental, 122; completion of railroad construction, 139

Treaty of Guadalupe-Hidalgo, 115-117, 119, 122, 125, 126, 129, 134
Tubac, 56-58, 63, 121, 122
Tumacacori, 54

Ulibarri, 49
Ulloa, Francisco de, 15, 55
United Farm Workers Organizing Committee, (UFWOC), 167
United Mexican American Students, (UMAS), 169
Ute, 24, 49, 96

vaquero, 77, 80
Vargas, Don Diego de, 47
Vasquez, Tiburcio, 132, 133
Villagra, Gaspar Perez de, 73
Villalobos, Ruy Lopez de, 32
Virgin de Guadalupe (The Brown Madonna), 163, 165
Viscaino, Sebastian, 34, 59, 60

War of 1812, 100
War with the United States, 106
War on Poverty Program, 150
water rights, 121, 129, 130
weaving, 72, 73
wetbacks, 150
Wichita, 18, 25, 27, 41
World War I (1914-1918), 144, 147
World War II (1939-1945), 149-151, 153, 160, 163

Ximines, Vincente T., 157
Xixime, 18

Yankee ships, 84; trader, 94
Yaqui, 18
Young, Brigham, 114, 115
Yuma Indians, 55, 63

Zacatecas, Mexico, 35
Zavala, Lorenzo de, 101
Zia, 47
"zoot suit riots," 153, 154
Zuñi, 11, 12, 15, 18-20, 36, 40